The Transformative Daf

MOSAICA PRESS

RABBI DANIEL FRIEDMAN

The Transformative Daf

Tractate Megillah

Published by Mosaica Press, Inc.
www.mosaicapress.com
info@mosaicapress.com

Dedicated in honour
of our beloved son and brother

Matvey / Matityahu

on the occasion of your bar mitzvah
June 2021/ Sivan 5781

Moshe, Anna, Semion,
and Aaron Kantor

BETH DIN ZEDEK
ECCLESIASTICAL JUDICATURE OF THE
CHICAGO RABBINICAL COUNCIL

בית דין צדק דק"ק שיקגו והגליל
דמועצת הרבנים דשיקגו

בס"ד

הרב גדלי' דוב שווארץ זצ"ל, ראב"ד מלפנים
RABBI GEDALIA DOV SCHWARTZ of blessed memory
Rosh Beth Din Emeritus

הרב ישראל מאיר קרנו זצ"ל, ראב"ד מלפנים
RABBI ISRAEL M. KARNO of blessed memory
Av Beth Din Emeritus

הרב חיים דוד רגנשברג זצ"ל, מייסד חב"ד"ץ
RABBI C. DAVID REGENSBERG of blessed memory

הרב יונה ריס, אב"ד
RABBI YONA REISS
Av Beth Din

הרב אברהם מרדכי אברמסון
RABBI ALAN M. ABRAMSON
Menahel

כ״ג ניסן, שנת חמשת אלפים תשפ״א

כבוד ידידי,

Our esteemed colleague Rabbi Daniel Friedman שליט״א has written a lucid and lyrical book, Daf YoMe, that extracts nuggets of wisdom and pearls of perspicacity from the pages of the Talmud. As an experienced and successful shul Rabbi, Rabbi Friedman has a special talent for connecting with his audience, whether through the written word or the spoken sermon, in a fashion which is (מחזיר)בתשובה so מעורר ליבין, capable of restoring a persons spiritual well-being, and intellectual appreciation of the Torah's values and teachings. One cannot help but be enriched by Rabbi Friedmans combination of psychological acuity, human compassion, and religious fervor.

ובכן אומר לגומרו גדולה התורה, שיעלה כתרה ויגדל מורא שמים בקרב גוים, ויזכו לרבים.

yona Reiss

מוסדות אור שמח מרכז טננבאום ע.ר. 58-00-21343-00

רח׳ שמעון הצדיק 22-28 ירושלים ת.ד. 18103
טל: 02-581-0315

Nissan 5781

MICHTAV BRACHA

Chazal say, "Great is learning because it leads to [virtuous] action" (*Kiddushin* 40b).
Ramban writes in his celebrated letter that after learning anything in Torah, one
should seek some way to apply that teaching to one's life. Every part of Hashem's
Torah is precious beyond measure, but many, perhaps most, of us have some
difficulty finding this application. While there are many passages in Tanach and
Talmud where the practical lessons are clear, with many others, the message is
obscure and elusive.

Rabbi Daniel Friedman has performed a truly valuable service in providing some
badly needed assistance. He has authored a book going through the 2,700 plus pages
of the Babylonian Talmud, extracting from each *daf* lessons that can be applied to real
life. Some stress practical behavior, such as fixing negative character traits and
acquiring and developing virtuous ones, others are inspirational, and still others
provide a broader philosophical perspective that can help us in our life's journey to
become true *avdei Hashem*. Those who study the *daf yomi* will walk away with
practical guidance that will elevate the *ruchniyus* in their lives; for those who do not
yet study the *daf*, there is the additional benefit of giving them a way to participate in
this wonderful global learning endeavor.

Rabbi Friedman deserves our heartfelt gratitude for producing a work that is so
helpful on both a practical and inspirational level. May he have much *hatzlachah* both
in the dissemination of this book and in all of his *avodas ha'kodesh*.

With Torah blessings,
Yitzchak A. Breitowitz
Rav, Kehillat Ohr Somayach, Yerushalayim

Table of Contents

Preface

Welcome to *Masechta Megillah*! While there are in fact five *Megillos*, this tractate deals with the most famous one: *Megillas Esther*. We all know the story of Purim. If we had to sum it up in a single phrase, what would it be?

V'nahafoch hu—It was transformed!

The *Megillah* says that when the Jews of Persia thought that all was lost, suddenly, everything was transformed. The greatest anti-Semite of the time had plotted to wipe out the entire Jewish people. But instead, he and his family perished.

The message of the *Megillah* is clear. Transformation is possible in the blink of an eye. When life seems bleakest, when the challenges have overwhelmed you, remember *v'nahafoch hu*. The Almighty is about to transform your life in an instant!

That's what *The Transformative Daf* is all about: first, maintaining our faith in Heaven's transformative ability; and second, maintaining our faith in our own personal transformative ability. No matter who you think you are, regardless of the story of your life until this point, you have the ability to completely transform the way you think, speak, and live your life!

The patron of this tractate is Dr. Moshe Kantor, one of the towering figures of world Jewry today. In addition to Moshe's countless philanthropic accomplishments, and his leadership in the fields of business, science, politics, and the arts, in 2020 he fulfilled an ancient prophecy. Our prophets spoke of the day when all the leaders of the nations of the earth would descend upon Jerusalem to honor the Jewish people.

Never in history has this come to pass. Not in the time of King David. Nor in the time of King Solomon. But Moshe Kantor made it happen. Seeing the problem of rising anti-Semitism across the globe, he had a vision: bring all the world's leaders together to make a united declaration against those who wish to destroy the Jewish people. I want to thank Moshe for extending the privilege to Rabbanit Batya and me, inviting us to join this exclusive, unforgettable gathering.

Thus, what better volume of *The Transformative Daf* to dedicate than *Megillah*? The Almighty works in extraordinary ways. Moshe didn't request this tractate specifically, but miraculously, Moshe's life's mission—combating anti-Semitism—is embodied in this particular volume. This dedication is Moshe and Anna's gift to their son Matvey on the occasion of his bar mitzvah. What an honor it was to share the pulpit with former Israeli Chief Rabbi Yisrael Meir Lau along with Britain's Chief Rabbi Ephraim Mirvis for the special event.

Mazal tov Matvey. May you follow in your parents' footsteps as leaders of Klal Yisrael, and may the words of this volume inspire you to lead a life of transformative Judaism!

Thank you to all the people who have a *chelek* in the *zechus* of this *sefer*. Of course, as always, the greatest appreciation goes to my dear wife and soul mate, Rabbanit Batya Yocheved, my rock and source of inspiration, guidance, and patience over the many years of *The Transformative Daf*. As Rabbi Akiva announced to his students: "What is mine and yours is truly hers."

My special dedication of this volume goes to our dear friends at Hampstead Garden Suburb Synagogue, London, UK. You are forever in our hearts. A huge thank you to Rabbis Yaacov Haber and Doron Kornbluth and the entire team at Mosaica Press for going above and beyond every step of the way.

And, finally, thank you to the Ribbono shel Olam for all the blessings in my life. I feel very humbled to be the vehicle for these teachings.

Rabbi Daniel Friedman
Menachem Av 5781
London

DAF 2

Country Air

n ancient times, there was a special dispensation for villagers to hear the *Megillah* reading earlier than the fourteenth of Adar, the actual day of Purim. Many villagers would enter the cities on Mondays and Thursdays when the Torah was read and the courts were open, as per the institution of Ezra the Scribe. Villagers did not have the skills to read the *Megillah* and they needed a townsman to read it for them on the Monday or Thursday prior to Purim.

Nevertheless, the practice ceased once the messengers of the High Court in Jerusalem no longer traveled throughout the countryside to inform the people when Pesach would occur. The Rabbis feared that the villagers would read the *Megillah* early and then count thirty days until Pesach. Their early start to Pesach would culminate in an early end to Pesach, causing them to eat chametz too soon!

Let's think about that prospect for a moment. Do we really believe people are so ignorant that because they would read the *Megillah* early they would therefore eat chametz early?

מְגִילָה נִקְרֵאת בְּאַחַד עָשָׂר בִּשְׁנֵים עָשָׂר בִּשְׁלֹשָׁה עָשָׂר בְּאַרְבָּעָה עָשָׂר
בַּחֲמִשָּׁה עָשָׂר לֹא פָּחוֹת וְלֹא יוֹתֵר כְּרַכִּין הַמּוּקָפִין חוֹמָה מִימוֹת יְהוֹשֻׁעַ בֶּן
נוּן קוֹרִין בַּחֲמִשָּׁה עָשָׂר כְּפָרִים וַעֲיָירוֹת גְּדוֹלוֹת קוֹרִין בְּאַרְבָּעָה עָשָׂר אֶלָּא
שֶׁהַכְּפָרִים מַקְדִּימִין לְיוֹם הַכְּנִיסָה: גְּמ' מְגִילָה נִקְרֵאת בְּאַחַד עָשָׂר מְנָלָן
מְנָלָן כִּדְבָעֵינַן לְמֵימַר לְקַמָּן חֲכָמִים הֵקֵילוּ עַל הַכְּפָרִים לִהְיוֹת מַקְדִּימִין לְיוֹם
הַכְּנִיסָה כְּדֵי שֶׁיִּסַפְּקוּ מַיִם וּמָזוֹן לַאֲחֵיהֶם שֶׁבַּכְּרַכִּים אָמַר רַבִּי יְהוּדָה אֵימָתַי

1

בִּזְמַן שֶׁהַשָּׁנִים כְּתִיקָנָן וְיִשְׂרָאֵל שְׁרוּיִין עַל אַדְמָתָן אֲבָל בִּזְמַן הַזֶּה הוֹאִיל
וּמִסְתַּכְּלִין בָּה אֵין קוֹרִין אוֹתָהּ אֶלָּא בִּזְמַנָּהּ.

רש״י: אבל בזמן הזה—שפסקו כל אלה וישראל נפרדו ולא יגיעו שלוחי
ב״ד אצלם הכל צופין למקרא מגילה ואומרים יום י״ד באדר קרינן המגילה
נשארו לאדר ט״ו יום וט״ו של ניסן עושין פסח ואם תקדים קריאתה יעשו
פסח לסוף שלשים יום של קריאה ונמצאו אוכלין חמץ בימים אחרונים
(ביום) של פסח.

Mishnah: The Megillah may be read on the eleventh, twelfth, thirteenth, fourteenth, and fifteenth of Adar, no earlier and no later. Walled cities from the time of Yehoshua bin Nun read on the fifteenth. Villages and big cities read on the fourteenth, but the villages may advance the reading to the day of gathering.

Gemara: The Megillah may be read on the eleventh for the following reason: The Sages were lenient toward the villagers to advance the reading to the day of gathering [Monday or Thursday] so that they would be available on Purim to supply their townsfolk brethren with their provisions of food and drink. Rabbi Yehudah taught: When was this dispensation in effect? Only during the days of yore when the calendar was determined by the Sanhedrin and Israel were dwelling on their land. But nowadays, since people would look [at this practice of reading early and get confused], we only read it at the proper time.

Rashi: Nowadays, when all Sanhedrin matters have ceased and the beis din's messengers would not reach them [to inform them of the declared Pesach date], everyone looks forward to the Megillah reading, knowing that Purim is on the fourteenth of Adar. Following Purim, people count fifteen days until the conclusion of the month of Adar and then a further fifteen to Pesach, which begins on the fifteenth of Nissan. If they were to read the Megillah on the eleventh, they might start their thirty-day count immediately, consequently beginning Pesach on the eleventh of Nissan and end up eating chametz on the final days of Pesach.

Rabbi Yaakov Fekete explains that the provisions offered by the villagers were more than mere food and drink.[1] There's something wholehearted and spiritual about country living. City folk are more materialistic in nature, whereas the country environment provides for a perspective that allows for greater spiritual connection.

How much thought do city dwellers give to the loaf of bread on the supermarket shelf? We expect that when we enter the store, it will be there. Maybe your favorite brand will be out of stock, and you might have to purchase a different one today. But the bread will always be there.

Contrast that with country folk. A farmer knows that if Hashem doesn't provide the rain on time, the crop this year will be less than optimal. Unexpected infestation could wreak havoc on the crops. A rodent outbreak in the granary will ruin everything. These factors are beyond human control. And so, when the farmer davens each morning, he thinks about every word and pours out his heart before the Almighty, beseeching Him that everything that day go as smoothly as possible.

Rabbi Fekete's idea offers a powerful new approach to understanding *Rashi's* explanation. For the country folk, Pesach is dependent upon Purim. Unlike city dwellers, the people living in the country live a life of spirituality and miracles. When city dwellers think of Purim, they focus primarily on Esther's excellent advocacy, which saved the Jews from annihilation. Almost as an afterthought, they recognize that it couldn't have been mere coincidence that she was in the right place at the right time. And so Hashem must have played an overarching role.

Not so the country folk. They see God's hand every step of the way through the *Megillah*. Miracle upon miracle upon miracle. When they think Purim, they think Pesach.

And that's the provision the country folk are making for the city dwellers. It's not just the bread and water. It's an attitude to Purim that we need to hear. They arrive and remind us of Hashem's daily miracles throughout our lives.

So, why did the early *leining* cease?

---

1   *Emes L'Yaakov.*

Sadly, due to the travails of the exile, we've now lost that country feeling. Instead of Purim being infused with Passoverness—the awareness of Hashem's hand in every aspect of our lives—we risk our Pesach being impacted by Purimity—the arrogance stemming from the attitude that we are in control, that it's our advocacy and efforts primarily that dictate our success. The puffery of chametz, the risen dough, is likened by our Sages to arrogance, the feeling that we are greater than we actually are. But the truth is, our feelings of haughtiness are full of hot air.

Now we understand *Rashi*'s warning that this attitude may lead to early chametz consumption. When our Purim is chametz-driven, based on our inflated sense of self-worth, we run the risk of entering Pesach with the same haughty attitude to our human control over life's affairs.

It's time to bring a little country spirit into your life. Every time you drink, every portion of food you consume, remember all the miracles that have brought you that sustenance. May you learn to breathe the country air into your entire being!

Guardian Angels

When Cyrus the Great came to power in Persia, he granted permission to the Jews to return to Jerusalem and rebuild the Holy Temple. The jubilation, however, was short-lived. During our absence from Israel, the land was inhabited by non-Jews who became known as Samaritans. Initially, they offered their assistance to rebuild. But then they turned on our people and sent a letter to the Persian authorities to have the permission that had been granted by Cyrus revoked.

At that time, Daniel and his associates were still in Babylonia, in the court of Nevuchadnetzar. When Daniel heard the terrible news that the Temple rebuilding had been canceled, he entered a state of mourning and fasting. It was amid his mourning period that he would receive a visit from the angel Gavriel, who informed him about the redemption that would take place at the End of Days.

וְרָאִיתִי אֲנִי דָנִיֵּאל לְבַדִּי אֶת הַמַּרְאָה וְהָאֲנָשִׁים אֲשֶׁר הָיוּ עִמִּי לֹא רָאוּ אֶת הַמַּרְאָה אֲבָל חֲרָדָה גְדוֹלָה נָפְלָה עֲלֵיהֶם וַיִּבְרְחוּ בְּהֵחָבֵא מַאן נִינְהוּ אֲנָשִׁים אָמַר רַבִּי יִרְמִיָה וְאִיתֵּימָא רַבִּי חִיָּיא בַּר אַבָּא זֶה חַגַּי זְכַרְיָה וּמַלְאָכִי וְאִינְהוּ עֲדִיפִי מִינֵּיהּ וְאִיהוּ עֲדִיף מִינַּיְיהוּ אִינְהוּ עֲדִיפִי מִינֵּיהּ דְּאִינְהוּ נְבִיאֵי וְאִיהוּ לָאו נְבִיא אִיהוּ עֲדִיף מִינַּיְיהוּ דְּאִיהוּ חֲזָא וְאִינְהוּ לָא חֲזוּ וְכִי מֵאַחַר דְּלָא חֲזוּ מַאי טַעְמָא אִיבְּעִיתוּ אַף עַל גַּב דְּאִינְהוּ לָא חֲזוּ מַזְלַיְיהוּ חֲזוּ אָמַר רָבִינָא שְׁמַע מִינַּהּ הַאי מַאן דְּמִיבְּעִית אַף עַל גַּב דְּאִיהוּ לָא חֲזֵי מַזְלֵיהּ חֲזֵי מַאי תַּקַּנְתֵּיהּ

5

לִיקְרֵי קְרִיאַת שְׁמַע וְאִי קָאֵים בִּמְקוֹם הַטֻּנֹּפֶת לִינְשׁוֹף לִינְשׁוֹף מִדּוּכְתֵּיה אַרְבַּע
גַּרְמִידֵי וְאִי לָא לֵימָא הָכִי עִיזָּא דְּבֵי טַבָּחֵי שַׁמִּינָא מִינַּאי.

רש"י: מזלייהו—שר שֶׁל כָּל אָדָם לְמַעְלָה.

"And I, Daniel, alone saw the vision; for the men who were
with me did not see the vision, but a great quaking fell upon
them, and they fled to hide themselves." Who were these men?
Rabbi Yirmiah [or some say, Rabbi Chiya bar Abba] said: These
were Chaggai, Zechariah, and Malachi. They were superior to
him in one way and he was superior to them in another. They
were superior to him because they were prophets, and he
was not a prophet. He was superior to them because he saw
the vision, and they did not see. If they did not see, why were
they frightened? Although they themselves did not see, their
mazal saw. Ravina says: From here we learn that one who
is suddenly afraid, even though he doesn't see anything, his
mazal sees. What is his remedy? He should read Shema. And
if he is standing in a place of filth, he should distance himself
four cubits from his location. And if he is unable, let him say
the following: The goat of the slaughterhouse is fatter than me.

Rashi: His mazal refers to the ministering angel above each
person.

We perceive most things around us through our physical eyes. That's
reality as we know it. But the actual reality is that there is much more
going on in the spiritual realm around us that we simply do not see. In
our age of radio waves and Wi-Fi signals, we all understand that there
are things in the atmosphere around us that are beyond our physical
eyes. So it's not difficult to appreciate the abundance of spiritual activity also taking place in the environment around us.

The *Ramchal* explains that *mazal* refers to the *neshamah*. We are all
imbued with a Divine soul that strives to elevate us with the performance of Hashem's service. He teaches that the *neshamah* primarily
utilizes the faculties of the body to experience this world.[1] And so it sees

---

1   *Adir Bamarom*, part 1.

most things via the medium of your eyes. Nevertheless, it is not entirely bound by the sensory perceptions of the body. It is able to see things imperceptive to the human eye. When you feel certain inexplicable sensations, it is your *neshamah* or *mazal* "seeing" these experiences in a way that goes beyond the physical bounds of your physical faculties.

Rabbi Menachem Zvi Taksin explains that the way to conquer fear arising from hidden spiritual forces is to overpower them with the fear of Hashem by reciting *Shema*.[2] Reminding yourself that Hashem is greater than any power in all the physical and spiritual worlds will allay all fears. Sometimes your introspection will lead to the realization that you're standing in a place of filth, that the inexplicable spiritual fear you're experiencing stems from certain behavioral decisions you need to leap away from. Other times, our souls are simply weighed down by excessive focus on material gain. Recognizing that loss of focus on spiritual pursuits, one should declare "the goat of the slaughterhouse is fatter than me." A goat might be driven to eat more to achieve greater longevity, but really all it is doing is prioritizing itself for the slaughterhouse. That declaration should serve as a stark reminder of what's important in life.

Rashi offers an alternative interpretation of *mazal*. He says that *mazal* refers to a person's guardian angel. You have an angel that guides you through life. In fact, as Rabbi Simon teaches: "Every single blade of grass has a corresponding *mazal* which strikes it and tells it to grow."[3] When that little voice tells you to act a certain way or avoid going down an improper path, that's your guardian angel directing you. Put differently, your guardian angel is striking you and telling you to grow. You might want to take the easy route, but your guardian angel constantly encourages you to seek the ideal path and become your very best.

Do you remember the time you were in the supermarket and needed garlic salt? You found fresh garlic and table salt. Just as you were nearing the checkout, you noticed they actually had what you came for: "garlic salt." What did you do next? Honestly, you were in a rush to get home.

2   *Orach Yesharim.*
3   *Bereishis Rabbah* 10:6.

So you could be forgiven for deciding to leave the fresh garlic and the table salt on a random shelf.

But then a little voice, your *mazal*, told you, "Not so fast! The right thing to do is to put those other products back where they belong." And you thought, "Come on now, the store-workers will figure it out. That's what they get paid to do!" And you went back and forth inside your head and heart until you finally made the ethical decision to return the items to their proper shelves.

Now, obviously the supermarket story is silly and rather insignificant compared to the big, important issues your *mazal* deals with. Like when your alarm goes off in the morning and your *mazal* says, "It's time to get up for minyan!" Or when your *mazal* tells you that Monday night *shiur* is probably a better use of your time than Monday night football. Or when you're doing business and an ethical question arises. You know nobody will catch your shortcut, but your *mazal* says, "Do the right thing!"

Your guardian angel is guiding you every step of the way. May you tune in to the little voice of your *mazal* and choose the path to life!

DAF 4

Living the Megillah

n his later years, Rav Aharon Leib Shteinman once heard about a *chessed* opportunity, which he insisted on performing. Knowing he wasn't young anymore, his family tried to dissuade him.

"You don't have the strength for it," they said to him.

"Listen," he replied, "most people have already gone to their eternal rest. If Heaven has left me in the land of the living, I am obligated to act for the sake of Heaven. If I am too lazy to perform, I will also be sent to my eternal resting place."

He then began to cry and added, "The Almighty has only given me goodness, and what have I ever given back to Him. Nothing at all! He even saved me, the only one in my entire family to survive the war. And what am I doing for Him?"[1]

מְגִילָה בְּשַׁבָּת לָא קָרִינַן מַאי טַעְמָא אָמַר רַבָּה הַכֹּל חַיָּיבִין בִּקְרִיאַת מְגִילָה (וּבִתְקִיעַת שׁוֹפָר) וְאֵין הַכֹּל בְּקִיאִין בְּמִקְרָא מְגִילָה גְּזֵירָה שֶׁמָּא יִטְּלֶנָּה בְּיָדוֹ וְיֵלֵךְ אֵצֶל בָּקִי לִלְמוֹד וְיַעֲבִירֶנָּה אַרְבַּע אַמּוֹת בִּרְשׁוּת הָרַבִּים וְהַיְינוּ טַעְמָא דְשׁוֹפָר וְהַיְינוּ טַעְמָא דְלוּלָב רַב יוֹסֵף אָמַר מִפְּנֵי שֶׁעֵינֵיהֶן שֶׁל עֲנִיִּים נְשׂוּאוֹת בְּמִקְרָא מְגִילָה.

רש״י: נשואות למקרא מגילה—לקבל מתנות האביונים ואי אפשר בשבת.

1   Horowitz, *Otzar Sippurim L'Mechanchim* 2:289.

One does not read the Megillah on Shabbos. What is the reason? Rabbah said: Everyone is obligated in the mitzvos of reading the Megillah and blowing the shofar, but not everyone is proficient in reading the Megillah. Therefore, the Sages decreed [that the Megillah is not read on Shabbos] lest one take it in his hand and go to an expert to learn, and he may carry it four amos in the public domain. And this is the reason for the shofar. And this is the reason for the lulav. Rav Yosef offered an alternative reason: Because the eyes of the poor are raised to the reading of the Megillah.

Rashi: The Megillah reading reminds them that they are about to receive matanos l'evyonim and that is not possible on Shabbos.

Why would the needy community members anticipate their charity on Shabbos? Surely, they know that money is *muktzeh* and they certainly couldn't spend the money on Shabbos. Why could we not read the *Megillah* and then give them the money after Shabbos? It hardly seems like a sufficient reason to read the *Megillah* on the wrong day.

Perhaps Rav Yosef's message is not addressed to the needy. It's directed to everyone else and their mitzvos of *Megillah* and *matanos l'evyonim*. The *Megillah* reading, just like every mitzvah, must be transformative. How could we perform the mitzvah and not be motivated immediately to help the needy? When Hashem saved our ancestors from annihilation, Mordechai and Esther asked themselves: How can we ever repay our Father in Heaven for His abundant loving-kindness? And how can we contrast our lives with the evil demonstrated by Haman? Let us make charitable giving a fundamental aspect of Purim. Consequently, a key element built into the *Megillah leining* is to inspire us to become better human beings. If we can't do that because it's Shabbos, then *Megillah* reading gets moved to a weekday.

The example designed by Mordechai and Esther should be our model for every mitzvah we do. Each time we engage in our service of Hashem, we need to ask ourselves how we've become better people for it. It's customary to give tzedakah at some point during davening. Many people make a declaration committing to the mitzvah of *ahavas Yisrael* as they give tzedakah at the start of *Shacharis*. If I'm about to ask Hashem to act charitably toward me, first I need to commit to acting charitably toward others.

Many of us, sadly, compartmentalize our mitzvos into those that are between me and Hashem and those that are between me and my fellow human beings. Certainly, those categories exist—as the two Tablets of the *Aseres Hadibros* attest to. But there is an essential connection between both categories of mitzvos. They are dependent upon one another—if the "God" mitzvos don't inspire you to fulfill the "man" mitzvos, then something is missing.

The Almighty gives us mitzvos to refine us, to make us better people. As you place your *tefillin shel yad* on your arm in the morning, you should be thinking about all the action mitzvos you're going to fulfill with your *yadayim* that day. If you put on tefillin and are not inspired to be the most ethical person in your corporate world, you should probably try on those tefillin once more. If learning Torah doesn't make you into a wiser, more thoughtful, and understanding person, then there's a certain dimension of your Torah study that is lacking.

Each year on Purim, many people *read* the *Megillah*. That wasn't Mordechai and Esther's point. They wanted us to *live* the *Megillah*. Each opportunity that you connect with Hashem through Torah, *tefillah*, and mitzvos, you must ask yourself how you have changed for the better. May every spiritual connection be transformative!

Intergenerational Leadership

Many of our Sages, such as the *Tur* and the Chafetz Chaim, are known by the famous *sefarim* they authored. Others, such as *Rashi* and the *Ramban*, are known by their personal name alongside their father's name. One of our great rabbis stands out with his appellation referring to his father's and grandfather's names. Rabbi Avraham ben HaRambam's life was so bound up with that of his famous father that the latter's entire name, which included his own father's name, Maimon, made it into the name by which he became known. What is the reason for his unique name reference?

At the age of forty-eight, the *Rambam* was blessed with the birth of his son. Despite his arrival late in the *Rambam's* life, he was immediately taken under his father's wing for all matters communal. From a young age, Avraham would sit next to the *Rambam*, watching as he dealt with Rabbinic questions, government relations, and community affairs. The *Rambam* understood how to guarantee that his child would be as dedicated to the community as he was. And indeed, Rabbi Avraham ben HaRambam succeeded his father as the head of the Jewish community in Egypt, filling his large shoes with wisdom and dedication.

אָמַר רַבִּי אֶלְעָזָר אָמַר רַבִּי חֲנִינָא רַבִּי נָטַע נְטִיעָה בְּפוּרִים וְרָחַץ בְּקָרוֹנָה שֶׁל
צִפּוֹרִי בְּשִׁבְעָה עָשָׂר בְּתַמּוּז וּבִקֵּשׁ לַעֲקוֹר תִּשְׁעָה בְּאָב וְלֹא הוֹדוּ לוֹ אָמַר
לְפָנָיו רַבִּי אַבָּא בַּר זַבְדָּא רַבִּי לֹא כָּךְ הָיָה מַעֲשֶׂה אֶלָּא תִּשְׁעָה בְּאָב שֶׁחָל
לִהְיוֹת בְּשַׁבָּת הֲוָה וּדְחִינוּהוּ לְאַחַר הַשַּׁבָּת וְאָמַר רַבִּי הוֹאִיל וְנִדְחָה יִדָּחֶה וְלֹא

12

הוֹדוּ חֲכָמִים קָרֵי עֲלֵיהּ טוֹבִים הַשְּׁנַיִם מִן הָאֶחָד וְרַבִּי הֵיכִי נָטַע נְטִיעָה בְּפוּרִים
וְהָתָנֵי רַב יוֹסֵף שִׂמְחָה וּמִשְׁתֶּה וְיוֹם טוֹב שִׂמְחָה מְלַמֵּד שֶׁאֲסוּרִים בְּהֶסְפֵּד
מִשְׁתֶּה מְלַמֵּד שֶׁאֲסוּר בְּתַעֲנִית וְיוֹם טוֹב מְלַמֵּד שֶׁאֲסוּר בַּעֲשִׂיַּת מְלָאכָה
אֶלָּא רַבִּי בַּר אַרְבֵּיסַר הֲוָה וְכִי נָטַע בַּחֲמֵיסַר נָטַע אִינִי וְהָא רַבִּי בִּטְבֶרְיָא הֲוָה
וּטְבֶרְיָא מוּקֶּפֶת חוֹמָה מִימוֹת יְהוֹשֻׁעַ בֶּן נוּן הֲוַאי אֶלָּא רַבִּי בַּר חֲמֵיסַר הֲוָה
וְכִי נָטַע בְּאַרְבֵּיסַר הֲוָה.

תוספות: והא רבי בטבריא הוה—נראה שהיה בימי אנטונינוס כשהיו יחד
כדאמר במס׳ ע״ז (דף י.) שרצה לשחרר בני טבריא ממס לפי שהיו תלמידי
חכמים דקאמר ליעביד טבריא קלניא.

Rabbi Elazar said in the name of Rabbi Chanina: Rebbi planted on Purim, and bathed in the Tzippori marketplace on the seventeenth of Tamuz, and wanted to uproot Tishah B'Av, but the Sages did not agree with him. Rabbi Aba bar Zavda responded: That wasn't the story. It was not a regular Tishah B'Av; rather, it was a Tishah B'Av that fell on Shabbos. Since the fast was pushed off, Rebbi felt that it should be pushed off completely [i.e., there should be no fast that year]. That was the proposal with which the Sages did not agree. Rabbi Elazar applied to him the verse, "Two [heads] are better than one." But how did Rebbi plant on Purim? Didn't Rav Yosef teach that the term "gladness" teaches that it is prohibited to eulogize on Purim, "feasting" teaches that it is prohibited to fast, and "Yom Tov" teaches that it is prohibited to perform labor? Rather, Rebbi was in a place that observed Purim on the fourteenth, and when he planted, he planted it on the fifteenth. Is that so? Wasn't Rebbi in Tiberias, and Tiberias was surrounded by a wall since the days of Yehoshua bin Nun? Rather, Rebbi lived in a place that observed Purim on the fifteenth, and when he planted, he planted it on the fourteenth.

Tosafos: Apparently it was during the time of his friendship with Antoninus, as it says in tractate Avodah Zarah that he sought to exempt the Tiberians from taxes because they were talmidei chachamim. As he said, "Make Tiberias a colony."

Seeking to understand where we find Rebbi's association with Tiberias, *Tosafos* concludes that the source is a conversation between Rebbi and his good friend, Roman Emperor Antoninus. In one exchange, the emperor tells Rebbi, "I have two wishes. First, I would like my son Asuerus to succeed me. Second, due to the abundance of Torah scholars here, I would like to make Tiberias a tax-free zone. But I am afraid that if I were to submit both of these requests to the Senate, they would fulfill but one. They would not fulfill both. What should I do?"

Rebbi presented a man riding on the shoulders of another man. He placed a dove in the hand of the upper man and said to the lower man, "Tell the upper man to let the dove fly forth from his hand!"

Antoninus understood, "Rebbi is teaching me: You should request that Asuerus succeed you and then Asuerus will, thereafter, make Tiberius a tax-free zone!"

How did Antoninus know that his son would ultimately fulfill his wishes?

A number of years ago, Rabbi J.J. Schacter visited Edmonton as scholar-in-residence for the Superstein Shabbaton. The Shabbaton was sponsored by Donny Superstein in honor of his parents, Jake and Ruth. Although he occasionally returns to Edmonton for business, nowadays Donny lives in Phoenix.

Sitting at the Shabbos table, Rabbi Schacter asked Donny about his family. At the time, Donny was divorced, but had a teenage son, Joey.

"Where's Joey?" asked Rabbi Schacter.

"He's in Phoenix with his mom," replied Donny. "He's normally with me on weekends, but he stayed with his mother this week because I came up for the Shabbaton."

"Donny," said Rabbi Schacter gently. "Did you ever think what an impression it would make on Joey to have him see how you are conducting your financial affairs? As a parent, the greatest impact you could make on your son is to bring him up close to watch you so that he can learn from and become involved in your philanthropic activities. Your role as a father is to demonstrate to Joey the true purpose of our material lives!"

How could Antoninus know that his son would fulfill his wishes? Rebbi's message was that the secret is to carry him upon his back. As long as he brought his son along for the ride, he could rest assured that his son would continue his life's mission and aspirations. From Rebbi to the *Rambam* to Rabbi Schacter, our Sages have always understood that the key to generational continuity of mission and purpose is immersion and osmosis of that mission and purpose during the lifetime of the older generation. If we bring our children along with us for the ride by demonstrating the responsibilities we are adopting, only then will they understand and appreciate the importance of the pursuits we hold dear.

Rav Yosi bar Choni teaches that there are two people that one does not envy in the world—one's student and one's child.[1] We all want to see our children not just succeed but soar to even greater accomplishments than we ourselves achieved. Rebbi's message to Antoninus, and Rabbi Schacter's message to Donny, was that your child is an extension of yourself. In your short lifetime, you can only achieve so much—start investing your communal aspirations in your child and your reach will fly like a dove, soaring way beyond what you've achieved in your limited time on Earth.

As community leaders, we are sometimes so caught up in communal matters, we forget to train our own children to be leaders. It's not easy to find the time. The shortcut is to involve them and let them watch and learn from their front-row seats to our lives.

Invest in your child's leadership abilities and qualities. Bring them into the conversation from an early age. Get them inspired to follow in your footsteps. May your leadership accomplishments continue to grow for generations to come!

---

1   *Sanhedrin* 105b.

Why Do We Covet?

F ollowing the territorial division of the Land of Israel between the tribes, the tribe of Zevulun concluded that the portion they had received was unfair. They turned their eyes Heavenward and said, "Master of the Universe! To my brothers You gave fields and vineyards, but to me You gave mountains and hills. To my brothers You gave lands, whereas to me You gave seas and rivers!"

Hashem replied, "That may be true, but all will need your resources, which will include the *chilazon*, the snail whose blue blood was used to dye tzitzis with the *techeiles* coloring. What's more, your portion will include other bounty, such as tuna and white glass. It will be a plentiful and fertile portion, a land overflowing with milk and honey!"

Zevulun responded, "Master of the Universe, who will inform me if others take them without permission?"

Hashem replied, "Anyone who takes these items from you without making payment will not prosper at all in his business."

"But still," muttered Zevulun, "I still don't have the kind of fields and vineyards that my brother Naftali has."

זְבוּלוּן מִתְרַעֵם עַל מִדּוֹתָיו הֲוָה שֶׁנֶּאֱמַר זְבוּלוּן עַם חֵרֵף נַפְשׁוֹ לָמוּת מַה טַעַם
מִשּׁוּם דְּנַפְתָּלִי עַל מְרוֹמֵי שָׂדֶה אָמַר זְבוּלוּן לִפְנֵי הַקָּדוֹשׁ בָּרוּךְ הוּא רִבּוֹנוֹ שֶׁל
עוֹלָם לְאַחַי נָתַתָּ לָהֶם שָׂדוֹת וּכְרָמִים וְלִי נָתַתָּ הָרִים וּגְבָעוֹת לְאַחַי נָתַתָּ לָהֶם
אֲרָצוֹת וְלִי נָתַתָּ יַמִּים וּנְהָרוֹת אָמַר לוֹ כּוּלָּן צְרִיכִין לָךְ עַל יְדֵי חִלָּזוֹן שֶׁנֶּאֱמַר
[עַמִּים הַר יִקְרָאוּ] וּשְׂפוּנֵי טְמוּנֵי חוֹל תָּנֵי רַב יוֹסֵף שְׂפוּנֵי זֶה חִלָּזוֹן טְמוּנֵי זֶה

16

טָרִית חוֹל זוֹ זְכוּכִית לְבָנָה אָמַר לְפָנָיו רִבּוֹנוֹ שֶׁל עוֹלָם מִי מוֹדִיעֵנִי אָמַר לוֹ
שָׁם יִזְבְּחוּ זִבְחֵי צֶדֶק סִימָן זֶה יְהֵא לְךָ כָּל הַנּוֹטֵל מִמְּךָ בְּלֹא דָּמִים אֵינוֹ מוֹעִיל
בִּפְרַקְמַטְיָא שֶׁלּוֹ כְּלוּם וְאִי סָלְקָא דַעְתָּךְ קִטְרוֹן זוֹ צִיפּוֹרִי אַמַּאי מִתְרַעֵם עַל
מִדּוֹתָיו וְהָא הַוְיָא צִיפּוֹרִי מִילְתָא דַעֲדִיפָא טוּבָא וְכִי תֵּימָא דְלֵית בַּהּ זָבַת
חָלָב וּדְבַשׁ וְהָאָמַר רֵישׁ לָקִישׁ לְדִידִי חֲזֵי לִי זָבַת חָלָב וּדְבַשׁ דְּצִיפּוֹרִי וְהַוְיָא
שִׁשָּׁה עָשָׂר מִיל עַל שִׁשָּׁה עָשָׂר מִיל וְכִי תֵּימָא דְלָא נְפִישָׁא דִידֵיהּ כְּדַאֲחוּהּ
וְהָאָמַר רַבָּה בַּר בַּר חָנָה אָמַר רַבִּי יוֹחָנָן לְדִידִי חֲזֵי לִי זָבַת חָלָב וּדְבַשׁ דְּכָל
אַרְעָא דְיִשְׂרָאֵל וְהַוְיָא כִּמְבֵּי כּוּבֵּי עַד אַקְרָא דְתוּלְבַּקְנֵי עֶשְׂרִין וְתַרְתֵּין פַּרְסֵי
אוּרְכָּא וּפוּתְיָא שִׁיתָא פַּרְסֵי אֲפִילּוּ הָכִי שָׂדוֹת וּכְרָמִים עֲדִיפָא לֵיהּ דַּיְקָא נָמֵי
דִּכְתִיב וְנַפְתָּלִי עַל מְרוֹמֵי שָׂדֶה שְׁמַע מִינַהּ.

Zevulun was resentful of its portion, as it is stated, "Zevulun was a people that jeopardized their lives to the death." What is the reason for their resentfulness? Because "Naftali was on the high places of the fields." Zevulun said before the Holy One, blessed be He, "Master of the Universe! To my brothers You gave fields and vineyards, whereas to me You gave mountains and hills; to my brothers You gave lands, whereas to me You gave seas and rivers..." And if you would say that Zevulun's portion did not have quality land flowing with milk and honey, didn't Reish Lakish say, "I myself have seen the land flowing with milk and honey around Tzippori, and it was sixteen mil by sixteen mil"? And if you would say that the part of his territory that flowed with milk and honey was not as vast as that of his brothers, the other tribes, didn't Rabbah bar bar Chana say that Rabbi Yochanan said, "I myself have seen the land flowing with milk and honey over all of Eretz Yisrael. And the size of the fertile land was like the distance from Bei Kovei to the fortress of Tulbakni, a total of twenty-two parasangs in length and six parasangs in width"? Even so, fields and vineyards were preferable to Zevulun. The language of the verse is also precise according to this explanation, as it is written: "And Naftali was on the high places of the field." Indeed, learn from here.

The Tenth Commandment declares, "You shall not covet your neighbor's house: you shall not covet your fellow's wife, or his male or female slave, or his ox or his ass, or anything that is your fellow's."[1] What causes a person to covet and want what someone else has? The story of Zevulun's conversation with God offers extraordinary insight into the tragedy of this common character flaw.

The Almighty has given different blessings to every person. The reason people covet is that they hone in on one particular blessing that somebody else has and wonder why Hashem wasn't as benevolent to them. Of course, He has been very gracious to them, but momentarily they manage to forget all the blessings He has bestowed upon them because they're so fixated on the one thing the other person has that they don't have.

Despite all the incredible bounty Zevulun possessed, all he could think about was Naftali's fields and vineyards. Never mind that Naftali had no *chilazon*, tuna, or white glass. Never mind that Naftali had nowhere near as much milk and honey. When you covet someone else's possessions, you don't look at what they don't have—all you can think about is what they do have that you don't.

The cure for jealousy is to think about all your blessings. Maybe the Almighty hasn't showered you with riches, but you've been blessed with good health. All the money in the world couldn't buy good health! Maybe you've been blessed with nice, respectful children. Isn't that worth thanking Hashem for? Maybe you've been blessed with a pleasant spouse, with whom you can share your innermost thoughts and feelings. Isn't that more wonderful that a fancy car?

There's a classic story told of Zalman, who was terribly upset with his lot in life. He looks around at his friends. Moshe's house has the most amazing view of the ocean. Yitzy's car turns heads. Shloimy is the CEO of a major company. One night, Zalmy has a dream. He finds himself walking through a huge field with a *"pekel,"* a sack on his back. Inside the *pekel* are his house, his car, his wife, his children, his medical records, the Torah he's learned and wisdom he's acquired. But also inside the *pekel* are all the challenges he has ever dealt with in his life.

---

1   *Shemos* 20:14.

As he makes his way toward the middle of the field, he sees, coming from various directions, Moshe, Yitzy, Shloimy, and dozens of other people whom he's met over the years. Suddenly, a voice booms, "Throw your *pekel* into the middle of the field!" He dutifully follows the instructions, and watches as everyone obeys the command. "Now, look around you," continues the Heavenly voice, "and choose the life with which you would rather have been blessed." In an instant, there's a rush for everyone to grab the *pekel* they believe contains the best life one could wish for.

Lo and behold, each participant takes the same *pekel* with which he arrived. Having gazed solely upon Moshe's house, Yitzy's car, and Shloimy's job, Zalmy realizes that he failed to appreciate the entire package of his blessings in life—and the less than attractive aspects of his friends' *pekelach*.

The Almighty has bestowed incredible blessing upon your life. When you simply focus on one aspect of your friend's possessions, you have no idea what the whole picture looks like. Think about all the blessings Hashem has given you. Your life is probably quite enviable. May you never take a single blessing for granted, and may you thank Hashem for your *pekel* in life!

Drinking on Purim

Rabbah and Rabbi Zeira celebrated their Purim feast together. In the midst of their rejoicing, they became intoxicated to the point that Rabbah arose and slaughtered Rabbi Zeira. The next day, Rabbah begged Heaven for mercy, and resurrected his friend.

The next year, Rabbah said to Rabbi Zeira, "Let's have our feast together again this Purim."

"My dear brother," Rabbi Zeira responded, shaking his head, "you and I know both know: miracles do not happen every day."

וּמַתָּנוֹת לָאֶבְיוֹנִים תָּנֵי רַב יוֹסֵף וּמִשְׁלוֹחַ מָנוֹת אִישׁ לְרֵעֵהוּ שְׁתֵּי מָנוֹת לְאִישׁ
אֶחָד וּמַתָּנוֹת לָאֶבְיוֹנִים שְׁתֵּי מַתָּנוֹת לִשְׁנֵי בְּנֵי אָדָם רַבִּי יְהוּדָה נְשִׂיאָה שַׁדַּר
לֵיהּ לְרַבִּי אוֹשַׁעְיָא אַטְמָא דְּעִיגְלָא תִּלְתָּא וְגַרְבָּא דְּחַמְרָא שָׁלַח לֵיהּ קַיְּימַתְּ
בָּנוּ רַבֵּינוּ וּמִשְׁלוֹחַ מָנוֹת אִישׁ לְרֵעֵהוּ וּמַתָּנוֹת לָאֶבְיוֹנִים רַבָּה שַׁדַּר לֵיהּ לְמָרֵי
בַּר מָר בְּיַד אַבַּיֵּי מְלֵא טַסְקָא דְּקַשְׁבָּא וּמְלֵי כָּסָא קִמְחָא דַּאֲבִשׁוּנָא אֲמַר
לֵיהּ אַבַּיֵּי הַשְׁתָּא אָמַר מָרִי אִי חַקְלָאָה מַלְכָּא לֶיהֱוֵי דִּיקּוּלָא מִצַּוְּארֵיהּ לָא
נָחֵית הֲדַר שַׁדַּר לֵיהּ אִיהוּ מְלֵא טַסְקָא דְּזַנְגְּבִילָא וּמְלֵא כָּסָא דְּפִלְפַּלְתָּא
אֲרִיכְתָּא אֲמַר אַבַּיֵּי הַשְׁתָּא אָמַר מָר אֲנָא שַׁדַּרִי לֵיהּ חוּלְיָא וְאִיהוּ שַׁדַּר לִי
חוּרְפָּא אֲמַר אַבַּיֵּי כִּי נְפַקִי מִבֵּי מָר הֲוָה שָׂבַעְנָא כִּי מְטַאי לְהָתָם קָרִיבוּ לִי
שִׁיתִין צָעֵי דְּשִׁיתִין מִינֵי קְדֵירָה וַאֲכַלִי בְּהוּ שִׁיתִין פְּלוּגֵי וּבִישׁוּלָא בַּתְרַיְיתָא
הֲוֵו קָרוּ לֵיהּ צְלִי קָדֵר וּבָעֵאי לְמִיכַס צָעָא אַבַּתְרֵהּ אֲמַר אַבַּיֵּי הַיְינוּ דְּאָמְרִי
אִינָשֵׁי כָּפֵין עַנְיָא וְלָא יָדַע אִי נָמֵי רְוִיחָא לִבְסִימָא שְׁכִיחַ אַבַּיֵּי בַּר אָבִין וְרַבִּי
חֲנִינָא בַּר אָבִין מַחְלְפִי סְעוֹדָתַיְיהוּ לַהֲדָדֵי אֲמַר רָבָא מִיחַיַּיב אִינִישׁ לְבַסּוּמֵי
בְּפוּרַיָּא עַד דְּלָא יָדַע בֵּין אָרוּר הָמָן לְבָרוּךְ מָרְדֳּכַי רַבָּה וְרַבִּי זֵירָא עָבְדוּ

סְעוּדַת פּוּרִים בַּהֲדֵי הֲדָדֵי אִיבַּסּוּם קָם רַבָּה שַׁחֲטֵיהּ לְרַבִּי זֵירָא לְמָחָר בָּעֵי
רַחֲמֵי וְאַחֲיֵיהּ לְשָׁנָה אֲמַר לֵיהּ נֵיתֵי מָר וְנַעֲבֵיד סְעוּדַת פּוּרִים בַּהֲדֵי הֲדָדֵי
אֲמַר לֵיהּ לָא בְּכָל שַׁעְתָּא וְשַׁעְתָּא מִתְרְחִישׁ נִיסָּא אֲמַר רָבָא סְעוּדַת פּוּרִים
שֶׁאֲכָלָהּ בַּלַּיְלָה לֹא יָצָא יְדֵי חוֹבָתוֹ מַאי טַעְמָא יְמֵי מִשְׁתֶּה וְשִׂמְחָה כְּתִיב
רַב אָשֵׁי הֲוָה יָתִיב קַמֵּיהּ (דְּרַב כָּהֲנָא) נְגַה וְלָא אֲתוּ רַבָּנָן אֲמַר לֵיהּ מַאי
טַעְמָא לָא אֲתוּ רַבָּנָן דִּלְמָא טְרִידֵי בִּסְעוּדַת פּוּרִים אֲמַר לֵיהּ וְלָא הֲוָה אֶפְשָׁר
לְמֵיכְלַהּ בְּאוּרְתָּא אֲמַר לֵיהּ לָא שְׁמִיעַ לֵיהּ לְמָר הָא דְּאָמַר רָבָא סְעוּדַת
פּוּרִים שֶׁאֲכָלָהּ בַּלַּיְלָה לֹא יָצָא יְדֵי חוֹבָתוֹ אָמַר לֵיהּ (אָמַר רָבָא הָכִי) [אִין]
תָּנָא מִינֵּיהּ אַרְבְּעִין זִימְנִין וְדָמֵי לֵיהּ כְּמַאן דְּמַנַּח בְּכִיסֵיהּ.

And gifts to the poor. Rav Yosef taught: "And of sending portions one to another" means two portions to one person. "And gifts to the poor" means two gifts to two people. Rabbi Yehudah Nesiah sent to Rabbi Oshaya the leg of a third-born calf and a jug of wine. Rabbi Oshaya sent him a message: You have fulfilled two mitzvos through us, our teacher—the mitzvah of "And sending portions one to another" and the mitzvah of "And gifts to the poor." Rabbah sent mishloach manos to Marei bar Mar in the hands of Abaye, consisting of a sack full of dates and a cupful of roasted flour. Abaye said to him: Now, Mari will say: "Even if a farmer becomes the king, the basket does not descend from his neck." Marei bar Mar sent back to him a sack full of ginger and a cupful of long peppers. Abaye said to him: The master will now say: "I sent him sweet items and he sent me pungent ones." Abaye said: When I left the house of the master, I was already satiated. However, when I arrived there, they served me sixty plates of sixty kinds of cooked dishes, and I ate sixty portions from each of them. The last dish was called pot roast, and I wanted to chew the plate afterward. Abaye said: This explains the popular saying: "The poor man is hungry and does not know it." Alternatively, "There's always room for dessert." Abaye bar Avin and Rabbi Chanina bar Avin would exchange their meals with each other. Rava said: A person is obligated to become so intoxicated on Purim until he does not know the difference between cursed

is Haman and blessed is Mordechai. Rabbah and Rabbi
Zeira celebrated their Purim feast together…"Miracles do not
happen every day." Rava said: A Purim feast that one ate at
night did not fulfill his obligation. What is the reason? The
Megillah states, "Days of feasting and simchah." Rav Ashi was
sitting before Rav Kahana, and it grew dark and the Sages
had not come. Rav Ashi said to him: What is the reason that
the Sages did not come today? Rav Kahana answered: Perhaps
they are preoccupied with the Purim feast. Rav Ashi said to
him: Wasn't it possible for them to eat the feast at night?
Rav Kahana said to him: Didn't the master learn that which
Rava said: A Purim feast that one ate at night did not fulfill
his obligation? Rav Ashi said to him: Did Rava say that? He
said to him: Yes. He then learned it from him forty times until
he remembered it so well that it seemed to him as if it were
placed in his purse.

What exactly happened between Rabbah and Rabbi Zeira on that
fateful Purim? The *Maharsha* explains that he didn't literally kill him.
It means that he pushed him to drink beyond his limits, placing his
life in potential danger. We've all been in situations like this at some
time or another. Our friends are drinking or engaging in other excessive
behavior, and we feel compelled to join in, pushing ourselves beyond
our limits. We wake up the next morning full of regret, thinking, "I can't
believe I succumbed to the peer pressure." That's why the following year
Rabbi Zeira gently declined the invitation.

But, if we look at the entire context of the Gemara in which this
strange story appears, an alternative idea begins to emerge. On Purim,
we have four special "M" mitzvos: *Megillah, Matanos l'evyonim, Mishloach*
Manos, and *Mishteh*, the feast. The Gemara begins by teaching that one
must send generous gifts to the poor on Purim so that they too can celebrate in style. The Gemara then transitions to *mishloach manos*, offering
a story where both mitzvos were fulfilled simultaneously. After that,
the Gemara offers other examples of rabbis who sent *mishloach manos*
to their friends on Purim.

The next transition is to the Purim feast, and the Gemara tells us that two rabbis exchanged their meals on Purim, suggesting that they were thereby able to fulfill both the mitzvos of *mishloach manos* and *mishteh*. But then Rava comments that one should drink on Purim until he doesn't know the difference between Mordechai and Haman. At first blush, that would seem to be quite a dangerous level of intoxication. And indeed, the subsequent story of Rabbah and Rabbi Zeira would support that understanding.

But then Rava's next teaching appears unrelated. Rava teaches that one does not fulfill one's *mishteh* obligation at night. And the Gemara tells a story of how long it took to drill down this idea of the right way to fulfill the mitzvah. It had to be repeated forty times!

Let's reexamine Rava's two lessons in light of the preceding narrative in the Gemara. When the miracle of Purim happened, Mordechai and Esther instituted a number of practices that would connect Jews in unity. Looking at the order of the Gemara, the first was gifts to the poor. The second was gifts to friends. And the third was to feast with one another. But with whom?

Rava teaches that the feasting should strive for a situation where one does not distinguish between Mordechai and Haman. Perhaps, he is impressing upon us that an important aim of the Purim festivities is to find people with whom to celebrate that we wouldn't ordinarily spend Shabbos and Yom Tov with. When we're simply drinking with friends, we run the risk of letting ourselves go beyond the limits of appropriate *simchah*. When we have people at the table who are not our best friends, we tend to be more cautious and avoid the type of excessive unruliness that Rabbah and Rabbi Zeira experienced.

And so Rava's next teaching is that we don't feast at night, because the *Megillah* states, "Days of feasting and *simchah*." True *simchah* doesn't mean letting ourselves go to the point where we lose control of our behavior. The Purim feast should be a religious celebration replete with *simchah*, *divrei Torah*, and demonstrations of brotherly love with those whom we might not ordinarily celebrate the rest of the year. Yes, we drink a little more than usual, because we've invited people who aren't our best friends and with whom we might need a little help to break the ice and take the edge off any previous occasions when we didn't see eye to eye.

But it shouldn't be a "nighttime" celebration. It's tempting to drink oneself to a level where you don't care what you say or do. If the purpose is to resolve differences and create a greater sense of Jewish unity, you can drink—but you must still maintain an appropriate level of awareness. You're tipsy enough to break down any barriers but still be completely aware and proud of your actions the next morning.

The bottom line is that the Purim feast has a special and unique purpose. It's the one day you should invite people who might not have been the most gracious to you during the past year. You might even feel they've acted a little Haman-like toward you. But it's Purim, the festival of Jewish unity in the face of adversity. The goal and challenge is to invite someone to your table who will allow you to feast until you don't differentiate between the Mordechais and Hamans in your life. And with God's help, maybe by the conclusion of the meal—with the help of a couple of *l'chaims*—you'll have put any prior issues behind you and you'll no longer view them as Haman characters.

This is not an easy task. We all have people we'd rather not bump into at someone else's home. And certainly, the last thing we'd want to do is invite them over to our own homes for Purim. It's much simpler to invite our close friends with whom we spend the other *Yamim Tovim*, but that misses the point and lowers the drinking from *simchah shel mitzvah* to an exercise in self-indulgence. May you accept the challenge to drink until you do not distinguish between Mordechai and Haman!

DAF 8

Giving Up Is a Good Thing

Achav was the most wicked king of Israel. Together with his pagan wife Izevel, he enticed the nation to worship the Baal and other idols. He murdered the true prophets of Hashem and replaced them with false prophets. During his reign, a famine struck the land for many years. In the third year of famine Hashem ordered Eliyahu HaNavi to appear before Achav and inform him that He would send rain upon the earth.

But first there would be a showdown. The prophets of the Baal would offer a sacrifice to their god upon Mount Carmel and Eliyahu would offer a sacrifice to Hashem. The big day arrived, and the Baal prophets prayed and engaged in all manner of ritual, to no avail. When it came time for Eliyahu's turn, he drenched the sacrifice and altar in water. A fire then came down from Heaven and devoured the sacrifice. And before they knew it, a cloudless sky had filled with rainclouds showering Hashem's blessing upon the earth.

In spite of all Achav's wicked deeds, our Sages teach that half of his sins were atoned for.[1] What was his special merit?

מַתְנִי׳ אֵין בֵּין הַמּוּדָּר הֲנָאָה מֵחֲבֵירוֹ לַמּוּדָּר מִמֶּנּוּ מַאֲכָל אֶלָּא דְּרִיסַת הָרֶגֶל וְכֵלִים שֶׁאֵין עוֹשִׂין בָּהֶן אוֹכֶל נֶפֶשׁ: גְּמ׳ הָא לְעִנְיַן כֵּלִים שֶׁעוֹשִׂין בָּהֶן אוֹכֶל

---

1   Sanhedrin 102b.

נֶפֶשׁ זֶה וְזֶה שָׁוִין: דְּרִיסַת הָרֶגֶל הָא לָא קְפְדֵי אִינָשֵׁי אָמַר רָבָא הָא מַנִּי רַבִּי אֱלִיעֶזֶר דְּאָמַר וִיתּוּר אָסוּר בְּמוּדָּר הֲנָאָה.

Mishnah: The difference between one for whom benefit from another is forbidden by vow and one for whom benefit from another's food is forbidden by vow is only with regard to stepping foot on his property, and with regard to borrowing utensils from him that one does not use in the preparation of food.

Gemara: With regard to the matter of utensils one uses in preparation of food, both this, one who vowed that any benefit is forbidden, and that, one who vowed that benefit from food is forbidden, are equal. Stepping foot? Aren't people not particular? Rava said: In accordance with whose opinion is this? Rabbi Eliezer, who said: vitur (giving up) is prohibited in the case of one for whom benefit is forbidden by vow.

In general, our Sages do not look kindly upon voluntary vows. Judaism does not call for abstinence; we are enjoined to partake of the pleasures of this world and sanctify them. Although vows of abstinence are permissible within the framework of halachah, our Rabbis have tended toward the sentiment that the mitzvos of the Torah already sufficiently restrain a person from overindulgence in this world.[2] Moreover, as Rabbi Eliezer declares in our Gemara, vows are not to be taken lightly. If one has made a vow, one must keep one's word without wavering in the slightest. One may not be *mevater* whatsoever.

From the perspective of *menschlichkeit*, placing oneself in a state where you cannot be *mevater* (give up) is highly problematic. *Vitur* or *vatranus* is a character trait that we should all strive for. What is *vatranus*? It's the attitude of not placing your own ego and selfhood in front of the needs and wants of another. It's such a powerful *middah* that our Sages teach that Achav was spared half his punishment because he was "*vatran b'mamono*," meaning that he readily gave of his own money

---

2   *Rambam, Hilchos De'os* 3:1.

to help others.[3] While he was certainly a tyrant, he still managed to provide for the needy, including the Torah scholars, during the years of the famine.

The trait of *vatranus* is a goal we must strive for throughout our lives, not only the financial realm. In every situation, we need to ask ourselves if our own *kavod* is getting in the way and then be the first to be *mevater*. Those situations arise in our marriages, in our relationships with siblings and other family members, at shul and in communal affairs, and at work.

For example, how often do we find people contesting the *amud* in shul? Each person feels that he has the right to be the *shaliach tzibbur* and he might even feel that it's not his own *kavod* at stake; it's the *kavod* of his parents who were *niftar*. When you find yourself in such a situation, here's what you need to know: your parents are in the *Olam HaEmes*. They don't want *machlokes* on their account. That certainly doesn't help their *neshamos*. The greatest assistance you can offer their *neshamos* is to be *mevater* on their account. That will give Hakadosh Baruch Hu such *nachas*, which will accrue even greater *zechuyos* to their *neshamos*!

Now, *vatranus* doesn't mean you let people take advantage of you. You need to have boundaries; it's unhealthy when others think they can walk all over you. But many issues we deal with are really not worth being obstinate about. If you can be the first to be *mevater* time and again, in situations that really make precious little difference in your life, people will come to develop an even deeper sense of respect for your strength of character.

We must aim throughout our lives to strike the balance between aggression and assertiveness. It's okay to assert your rights and needs; in fact, it's the right thing to do. But most situations call for *vatranus*, and even when you feel you shouldn't be *mevater*, you still need to ensure you act in a polite and non-aggressive manner. May you strive always to be the first to be *mevater*!

---

3   *Sanhedrin* 102b.

Removing the Difficult Bits from the Torah

King Ptolemy of Egypt once gathered seventy-two Jewish elders into seventy-two separate chambers and did not tell them for what purpose he had gathered them. He entered each room and said, "Translate the Torah of your teacher Moses into Greek for me."

The Almighty placed wisdom into the heart of each one and they all reached the same conclusions. Every time the literal translation would have left the reader with a misunderstanding of the true meaning of the text, which could have had negative ramifications for the Jewish people, they amended it. Miraculously, despite having no contact with one another, they were able to work in unison to ensure that the Torah would not be misconstrued by heretics for their idolatrous purposes.

My first encounter with Christian missionaries was as a young teenager in Sydney. One of the local bus drivers, Tuvia, was a "Messianic Jew." Tuvia was the friendliest bus driver in Bondi. He would welcome every passenger that boarded his bus, and proceed to give a running commentary en route, as if he were operating a tour bus. Inevitably, despite being a local, you learned something new about the area from Tuvia each time you traveled with him.

But Tuvia was a Messianic, and Messianics have an agenda. It wasn't just Bondi sights he wanted to teach. Seeing my yarmulke, Tuvia didn't hold back as he attempted to show me the light of his heretical beliefs. Looking back, I wonder how appropriate it was for him to be harassing his thirteen-year-old passenger with theological questions. But, at the time, I took it in stride and researched and responded to his provocations.

The first question he posed to me was the meaning of the verse, "Let us make man in our image as in our likeness." Clearly, said Tuvia, there was more than one Divine being that created man—an early prefiguration of Christian doctrine.

But I was far from the first Jew who had to deal with these taunts. As they sat in King Ptolemy's chambers, the Elders of Israel already anticipated such contentions. How did they respond?

מַעֲשֶׂה בְּתַלְמַי הַמֶּלֶךְ שֶׁכִּנֵּס שִׁבְעִים וּשְׁנַיִם זְקֵנִים וְהִכְנִיסָן בְּשִׁבְעִים וּשְׁנַיִם
בָּתִּים וְלֹא גִּילָּה לָהֶם עַל מָה כִּינְסָן וְנִכְנַס אֵצֶל כָּל אֶחָד וְאֶחָד וְאָמַר לָהֶם
כִּתְבוּ לִי תּוֹרַת מֹשֶׁה רַבְּכֶם נָתַן הַקָּדוֹשׁ בָּרוּךְ הוּא בְּלֵב כָּל אֶחָד וְאֶחָד עֵצָה
וְהִסְכִּימוּ כּוּלָּן לְדַעַת אַחַת וְכָתְבוּ לוֹ אֱלֹקִים בָּרָא בְּרֵאשִׁית אֶעֱשֶׂה אָדָם
בְּצֶלֶם וּבִדְמוּת וְכָתְבוּ לוֹ אֶת צְעִירַת הָרַגְלַיִם וְלֹא כָּתְבוּ לוֹ אֶת הָאַרְנֶבֶת
מִפְּנֵי שֶׁאִשְׁתּוֹ שֶׁל תַּלְמַי אַרְנֶבֶת שְׁמָהּ שֶׁלֹּא יֹאמַר שָׂחֲקוּ בִּי הַיְּהוּדִים וְהִטִילוּ
שֵׁם אִשְׁתִּי בַּתּוֹרָה.

King Ptolemy once assembled seventy-two Jewish Elders...
The Holy One, blessed be He, placed wisdom in the heart
of each and every one, and they all agreed to one common
understanding. And they wrote for him, "God created
in the beginning" [reversing the order so that it was not
misinterpreted as "Bereishis created God"]. And they wrote,
"I shall make man in image and in likeness" [rather than, "Let
us make man in our image as in our likeness"]...And [in the list
of nonkosher animals] they wrote for him, "The short-legged
creature," and they did not write for him, "And the rabbit,"
since the name of Ptolemy's wife was Rabbit, so that he would
not say, "The Jews have mocked me and inserted my wife's
name in the Torah."

In an effort to ensure the Torah's message wouldn't be distorted, the seventy-two Elders fine-tuned their translations in various places throughout the Torah. Let's explore a sample of their teachings.

The first reframing offered by the Elders is the very first phrase of the Torah, "In the beginning, God created," which was switched around to, "God created in the beginning." Rav Chanoch Gevhard describes the difference between the Jewish perspective on the Divine versus that of the nonbeliever.[1] Already, before we open up the Torah, our faith is rock solid. Our belief in Hashem precedes the first word. By contrast, the nonbeliever needs to be persuaded of Hashem's providence by encountering Him immediately upon opening the Torah. In other words, the Gemara's message to us is that our commitment to Heaven must be complete before we even begin to seek to understand. Just like we declared, *"Naaseh v'nishma"* prior to receiving the Torah, our entire approach to Yiddishkeit must be one of complete faith and unquestioning commitment prior to any inquiry.

In the second amendment, the Elders changed the plural "Let us make man" to the singular form, fearing that Ptolemy would infer that there were multiple deities who made man together. The *Ramban* explains that God fashioned everything in this world from the physical matter He had created. Everything was created from the earth, except man. When it came time to create human beings, God turned to the earth and invited heaven and earth to unite in the creation of man.

We are not physical beings. We are not spiritual beings. We are a unique combination of heaven and earth. Each human being consists of body and soul. Every moral choice we make is an opportunity to transcend this world. There is, however, a difference between Jews and non-Jews, which necessitated an amendment to the text in order to avoid confusion. The difference lies in our ability to sanctify this world and transform the physical into the spiritual.

Every human being has the ability to perform Divinely inspired acts and make this world a better place. Jewish or not, every act of kindness

---

1   *Shiurim B'Haggados Chazal*, p. 24.

and every charitable activity brings delight to our Father in Heaven. Nevertheless, the impact of the Jewish people upon the world is more profound.

When the Torah was given, the world changed. It wasn't our performance of mitzvos; our Sages teach that our forefathers kept the Torah even prior to the sixth of Sivan 2448. What changed on that day? The Midrash offers a parable of two nation-states with closed borders between them. That was the situation between heaven and earth until the Torah was given. On that day, the borders opened. Heaven could descend to earth and earth could ascend to heaven.[2]

Practically speaking, what happened was that on that day, we were given special powers to draw down the Divine into this physical world and transform the mundane into the spiritual. We can now take a piece of cow hide and some ink and elevate it to the status of a *Sefer Torah*. All of a sudden, if that *Sefer Torah* drops to the floor, God forbid, it will be customary to fast. Why? To the uninitiated eye, it's nothing but cow skin. But we know that it's so much more. It has now been transformed into a spiritual entity. And that gift to transform the physical into the spiritual was given to our people. That's why the "Let us make man" call to heaven and earth is directed specifically toward us and would have made no sense to Ptolemy.

Returning to King Ptolemy's chambers for one final example, let's skip ahead to the amendment of the king's wife's name, "Rabbit." Why did the Elders see fit to change that translation? And what message did the Gemara seek to convey by providing that specific example to us?

Sometimes, when we're learning Torah or doing mitzvos, we'll encounter things we personally find uncomfortable. It's tempting to want to change those bits to suit our own comfort and sensibilities. But we don't do that. The Gemara uses the inane example of the king's wife's name to demonstrate how absurd it is to start changing the Torah to suit our personal feelings.

---

2   *Shemos Rabbah* 12:3.

We adhere to Torah and mitzvos not because it makes us feel good, but because it is the Divine word. The Torah is Hashem's proclamation. Most of the time, we appreciate the incredible blessing that a life of Torah and mitzvos provides. But when, on occasion, we struggle with the Torah's message, we must know that it's not the Torah that is imperfect, it is us. The Torah is absolutely perfect; if we fail to appreciate the Torah's message, we must work harder to come to terms with Hashem's holy guidebook.

The Torah might need to be repackaged for the nations of the world so they will not misinterpret it and use it against us. But we are *maaminim b'nei maaminim*. We trust Hashem's word even when we don't immediately understand it. Our response is to toil until we arrive at the pure meaning of the Torah. May you forever embrace the Torah on Hashem's terms!

Don't Look Back

The angels have arrived in Sodom to inform Lot and his family of the impending disaster. After failing to convince his married daughters to flee the area, the angels tell him, "Arise, take your wife and your two daughters who are here, lest you perish because of the iniquity of the city."

But Lot and his family tarry, and so the angels must take hold of their hands and whisk them out of the city. As they're taking them out, the angels warn them, "Flee for your life, do not look behind you, and do not remain anywhere in the plain. Flee to the mountain, lest you perish."

Hashem then causes fire and brimstone to rain down upon Sodom and Amorah, turning over the cities and the entire plain, destroying all the inhabitants of the cities along with the vegetation on the ground. But just then, as they're fleeing for their lives, Lot's wife can't help herself. She turns around to take a peek at what's happening and is immediately transformed into a pillar of salt.

וַיְהִי בִּימֵי אֲחַשְׁוֵרוֹשׁ אָמַר רַבִּי לֵוִי וְאִיתֵּימָא רַבִּי יוֹנָתָן דָּבָר זֶה מָסוֹרֶת בְּיָדֵינוּ מֵאַנְשֵׁי כְּנֶסֶת הַגְּדוֹלָה כָּל מָקוֹם שֶׁנֶּאֱמַר וַיְהִי אֵינוֹ אֶלָּא לְשׁוֹן צַעַר וַיְהִי בִּימֵי אֲחַשְׁוֵרוֹשׁ הָיָה הָמָן וַיְהִי בִּימֵי שְׁפֹט הַשּׁוֹפְטִים הָיָה רָעָב וַיְהִי כִּי הֵחֵל הָאָדָם לָרֹב וַיַּרְא ה' כִּי רַבָּה רָעַת הָאָדָם וַיְהִי בְּנָסְעָם מִקֶּדֶם הָבָה נִבְנֶה לָנוּ עִיר וַיְהִי בִּימֵי אַמְרָפֶל עָשׂוּ מִלְחָמָה וַיְהִי בִּהְיוֹת יְהוֹשֻׁעַ בִּירִיחוֹ וַחַרְבּוֹ שְׁלוּפָה בְּיָדוֹ וַיְהִי ה' אֶת יְהוֹשֻׁעַ וַיַּמְעֲלוּ בְּנֵי יִשְׂרָאֵל וַיְהִי אִישׁ אֶחָד מִן הָרָמָתַיִם כִּי אֶת חַנָּה

אָהֵב וַה' סָגַר רַחְמָה אָמַר רַב אָשֵׁי כָּל וַיְהִי אִיכָּא הָכִי וְאִיכָּא הָכִי וַיְהִי בִּימֵי אֵינוֹ אֶלָּא לְשׁוֹן צַעַר.

"And it was (va'yehi) in the days of Achashveirosh." Rabbi Levi said, and some say that it was Rabbi Yonasan: This matter is a tradition that we received from the members of the Great Assembly. Anywhere that va'yehi is stated, it is a term indicating nothing other than impending trouble. "And it was in the days of Achashveirosh," [and then] there was Haman. "And it was in the days when the judges ruled" introduces a period when there was famine. "And it was when men began to multiply" is followed by the verse, "And the Lord saw that the wickedness of man was great in the earth." "And it was as they journeyed from the east" is followed by, "Come, let us build us a city." "And it was in the days of Amrafel" led to "They made war." "And it was, when Yehoshua was by Jericho" led to "With his sword drawn in his hand." "And the Lord was with Yehoshua" and afterward, "But the Children of Israel committed a trespass." "And it was that there was a certain man of Ramasayim" is followed by, "For he loved Chanah, but the Lord had closed up her womb..." Rav Ashi taught: With regard to every instance of va'yehi alone, there are some that portend trouble, and there are some that do not. However, wherever the phrase "and it was in the days of (va'yehi bi'yemei)" is used, it is nothing other than a term of impending trouble.

According to Rabbi Levi, anytime the Torah uses the phrase "and it was," it's a sign of trouble. Rav Ashi maintains that in order to warn of impending misfortune, the text must read "and it was in the days of." What's so concerning about these phrases?

There's a wonderful young man I know. Isaac has a great personality. He is dedicated to Torah and mitzvos and is active in the community. He just has one little problem—his failure to move his life forward. He's pushing thirty and still living at home with his parents. He's hesitant to date because he feels he doesn't have anything substantial to show for himself.

"I could've been a doctor," he told me one day. "My life would've been different if I'd gone to medical school."

"So why don't you go now?" I asked him.

"Oh, it's too late for that now. I should've done it years ago," was his response.

When you live your life by, "And it was," you are asking for trouble. Too many people think about what they should've done, what would've been and what could've happened, instead of looking forward to what they should do and what they could become if only they would look ahead. If you want to achieve happiness and success in life, the key is to stop looking backward.

Rav Ashi suggests a slightly different emphasis. The problem, he says, is not about saying "and it was," but thinking constantly "and it was in the days of." Some people don't regret their past. Instead they regret their present, looking back on the past with romanticized nostalgia about how things were so much better "back in the day."

That was Lot's wife's problem. As they were leaving Sodom, Lot and his family had only one command to obey. Just keep looking forward. Don't look back. Lot's wife was unable to let go of her past life in Sodom.

Is your ability to become your very best being constrained by your ties to the past? Do you find yourself hampered by a mindset of how your life could have turned out had you made different decisions along the way? Or can you not help but compare your situation today to an idealized memory of days long ago?

It's time to stop living in the past. As the classic cliché goes, "Yesterday is history, tomorrow's a mystery. Today's a gift—that's why it's called the present!" The only time of your life you can truly impact is right now. The past is past, and you don't know what tomorrow will bring. When you spend your life caught in the past or worrying about the future, you lose the gift of the present.

Rabbi Yehoshua ben Levi once met Eliyahu HaNavi. He asked him when Mashiach would arrive.

"Go and ask him," he replied, "he appears among the lepers at the gates of Rome."

Rabbi Yehoshua found Mashiach and asked him when he was coming.

"Today," he replied. Rabbi Yehoshua waited with great anticipation all day long. But nothing happened.

Disappointed, he returned to Eliyahu and told him about his exchange with Mashiach. "He lied to me!" exclaimed Rabbi Yehoshua to the prophet.

"No, he didn't," responded Eliyahu. "He was referring to the verse in *Tehillim* (95:7), 'Today, if you heed His voice.'"[1]

Today is the first day of the rest of your life. Today's the day to heed Hashem's voice, the voice that sent you on a mission into this world to prosper spiritually, materially, and indeed throughout every facet of your life. May you never look back, and may you achieve your very best!

---

1   *Sanhedrin* 98a.

Keeping Up Appearances

When Achashveirosh first ascended the Persian throne, he was concerned about the fulfillment of a prophecy from Yirmiyahu. After seventy years, declared the prophet, the Jews would return to the Land of Israel. He wasn't the first to worry about Yirmiyahu's words. Belshatzar, the king of Babylonia, had expressed similar concerns. And so he brought in his actuarial team and they created a statistical model: forty-five years of Nevuchadnetzar, and twenty-three of Evil-Merodach, and two of his own, for a total of seventy years, had passed without redemption. Concluding that Yirmiyahu's prophecy would no longer be fulfilled, Belshatzar took out the vessels of the Holy Temple and began to use them, publicly flaunting his derision of Heaven. But that night, a coup took place and he was slain.

Aware of the story of his predecessor, Achashveirosh said to himself, "Belshatzar miscalculated and erred. I too will calculate, but I will not err. Yirmiyahu didn't say, 'Seventy years for the kingdom of Babylonia.' He said, 'Seventy years for Babylonia,' meaning seventy years of the exile of Babylonia. How many years are still lacking from the seventy years? Eight years." He calculated, inserting in their stead the third year of Belshatzar, five years of Darius and Cyrus, and two years of his own, bringing the total to seventy. Once he saw that seventy years had been completed, and the Jewish people were still not redeemed, he said,

37

"Now they will certainly not be redeemed. Therefore, I will take out the vessels of the Holy Temple and use them."

בְּיָמִים הָהֵם כְּשֶׁבֶת הַמֶּלֶךְ וּכְתִיב בַּתְרֵיהּ בִּשְׁנַת שָׁלֹשׁ לְמָלְכוֹ אָמַר רָבָא מַאי
כְּשֶׁבֶת לְאַחַר שֶׁנִּתְיַישְׁבָה דַעְתּוֹ אָמַר בֵּלְשַׁצַּר חַשֵׁב וּטְעָה אֲנָא אֲנָא חָשֵׁיבְנָא
וְלָא טָעֵינָא מַאי הִיא דִכְתִיב כִּי לְפִי מְלֹאת לְבָבֶל שִׁבְעִים שָׁנָה אֶפְקוֹד
אֶתְכֶם וּכְתִיב לִמְלֹאות לְחָרְבוֹת יְרוּשָׁלַם שִׁבְעִים שָׁנָה חַשּׁוֹב אַרְבְּעִין וַחֲמֵשׁ
דִּנְבוּכַדְנֶצַּר וְעֶשְׂרִים וּתְלַת דֶּאֱוִיל מְרוֹדַךְ וְתַרְתֵּי דִּידֵיהּ הָא שִׁבְעִים אַפֵּיק
מָאנֵי דְּבֵי מַקְדְּשָׁא וְאִשְׁתַּמֵּשׁ בְּהוֹ הַיְינוּ דְּקָאָמַר לֵיהּ דָּנִיאֵל וְעַל מָרֵי שְׁמַיָּא
הִתְרוֹמַמְתָּ וּלְמָאנַיָּא דִי בַיְתֵיהּ הַיְתִיו קָדָמָךְ וּכְתִיב בֵּיהּ בְּלֵילְיָא קְטִיל
בֵּלְשַׁצַּר מַלְכָּא [כַּשְׂדָּאָה] וּכְתִיב וְדָרְיָוֶשׁ מָדָאָה קַבֵּל מַלְכוּתָא כְּבַר שְׁנִין
שִׁתִּין וְתַרְתֵּין אָמַר אִיהוּ מִיטְעָא טָעֵי אֲנָא אֲנָא חָשֵׁיבְנָא וְלָא טָעֵינָא מִי כְתִיב
לְמַלְכוּת בָּבֶל לְבָבֶל כְּתִיב מַאי לְבָבֶל לְגָלוּת בָּבֶל כַּמָּה בְּצִירָן תַּמְנֵי חֲשֵׁיב
וְעַיֵּיל חִילּוּפַיְיהוּ חֲדָא דְּבֵלְשַׁצַּר וַחֲמֵשׁ דְּדָרְיָוֶשׁ וְכוֹרֶשׁ וְתַרְתֵּי דִּידֵיהּ הָא
שִׁבְעִין כֵּיוָן דַּחֲזֵי דִּמְלוֹ שִׁבְעִין וְלָא אִיפְּרוּק אָמַר הַשְׁתָּא וַדַּאי תּוּ לָא מִיפַּרְקִי
אַפֵּיק מָאנֵי דְּבֵי מַקְדְּשָׁא וְאִשְׁתַּמֵּשׁ בְּהוֹ.

"In those days when the king sat," and afterward it is written, "In the third year of his reign." Rava said: What is the meaning of "when he sat" (k'sheves)? It means after his mind was settled (she'nisyashvah) [and he had overcome his anxiety with regard to the redemption of the Jewish people]. He said: Belshatzar calculated and erred. I will calculate, but I will not err. What is this calculation? As it is written, "After seventy years are accomplished for Babylonia I will remember you," and it is written, "That He would accomplish for the desolations of Jerusalem seventy years." He calculated: Forty-five years of Nevuchadnetzar, and twenty-three of Evil-Merodach, and two of his own, for a total of seventy. He therefore said: I will take out the vessels of the Holy Temple and use them. This is that which Daniel said to him, "But you have lifted yourself up against the Lord of Heaven; and they have brought the vessels of His House before you." And it is written, "On that night Belshatzar, the king of the Chaldeans, was slain." And it states, "And Darius the Mede received the kingdom, being about sixty-two years old." Achashveirosh said: He erred. I will

calculate, but I will not err...I will take out the vessels of the
Holy Temple and use them.

When it comes to our service of Heaven, we all have little things
we struggle with. Some of them are very personal and we know that
we're far from perfect. And we're able to keep those struggles behind
closed doors, knowing that we'll achieve self-mastery in good time.
And that's okay because nobody is perfect. We're all working to become
better Jews.

Maybe you pride yourself on not having a TV at home. That might be
true, but you know and God knows that you do watch the odd movie
on Netflix. Or maybe you are proud of your family's commitment to
keeping *yashan*. All the bread you purchase has come from last year's
crop, just as the Torah prescribes. But then there's the small matter of
those irresistible cookies that you occasionally can't help but indulge
in, right?

One day you tell yourself, "Who am I kidding? I know I'm eating the
cookies. God knows I'm eating the cookies. It's time to quit this hypoc-
risy and just be honest with myself. I don't actually keep *yashan*." And
so, you drop the whole *yashan* facade. Now you're eating all those cakes
and cookies of which you always dreamed.

I've chosen a bit of a comical example to bring out the idea in a way
that is relatable, but consciously not too pushy. Everyone knows for
himself where he's up to in life and what he considers to be a vice or
a virtue. The key element in the story is the moment a person decides
that his vice is no longer worth hiding from the world.

Why were Belshatzar and Achashveirosh so eager to use the Temple
vessels? They had all the utensils in the world at their disposal. Were all
those utensils not sufficient for their needs?

Take a closer look at the wording of the Gemara. We're not simply
informed that these wicked kings used the Temple vessels. The Gemara
emphasizes that each one declared, "I will *take out* the vessels of the
Holy Temple and use them." We don't know how they acted behind
closed doors; that's immaterial. What we do know is that each time our
Sages censure them for their brazenness, they make it clear that these

kings not only acted inappropriately, but they put their acts on display for all to see. In fact, so desperate were they to publicize and normalize their behavior, they even made the Jews eat off the vessels as well.

Of course, we're not wicked rulers like Belshatzar and Achashveirosh, but we do have behaviors that are best kept behind closed doors, between us and God. When you bring those behaviors out into the open, it means you've abandoned all hope of ever improving in those areas of your spiritual life.

The story is told of the fellow from New York who gets a job in middle America. He arrives in town to find that the only synagogue is Conservative. He's always been a shul-goer and he decides to give the new community a try. After all, he tells himself, he's not that *frum*, so why should he limit himself denominationally? So Shabbos morning, he gets into his car, as he's always done, and heads in the direction of the synagogue. Once Waze has brought him to his destination, he drives around the corner and finds a parking spot. He then heads back over to the synagogue by foot.

The security guard welcomes him, but then looks at him quizzically, "Sir, you know, I did see you drive past five minutes ago. You didn't have to park on the street. We're a Conservative synagogue. We have a wonderful, spacious parking lot alongside our building!"

"Yes, I realize," replies the New Yorker, "but I'm Orthodox."

You might not yet completely be at a level of observance that aligns with your perspectives on Torah and mitzvos. Or you might even have a pretty decent track record when it comes to *frumkeit*; it's just the occasional *taavah* that's not quite right. But the main thing is that you know where you'd like to be. May you keep those inner struggles between you and Hashem so that one day you can become the Jew you know you truly are!

Shabbos Is Not the Seventh Day

A chashveirosh had imbibed a little too much. It was Shabbos afternoon and he was feasting with his closest friends, engaged in a deep philosophical debate…

"Those women from Media are the most beautiful," one fellow began.

"What are you talking about?" cried his friend, "I say, Persians."

"You're both wrong," Achashveirosh responded, "mine is neither Median nor Persian, but Chaldean. Do you want to see for yourselves?"

"Sure," they replied, "just make sure we're able to make a clear judgment. She should be unattired."

בַּיּוֹם הַשְּׁבִיעִי כְּטוֹב לֵב הַמֶּלֶךְ בַּיַּיִן אַטּוּ עַד הַשְׁתָּא לָא טָב לִבֵּיהּ בְּחַמְרָא אֲמַר רָבָא יוֹם הַשְּׁבִיעִי שַׁבָּת הָיָה שֶׁיִּשְׂרָאֵל אוֹכְלִין וְשׁוֹתִין מַתְחִילִין בְּדִבְרֵי תוֹרָה וּבְדִבְרֵי תִשְׁבָּחוֹת אֲבָל אוּמּוֹת הָעוֹלָם שֶׁאוֹכְלִין וְשׁוֹתִין אֵין מַתְחִילִין אֶלָּא בְּדִבְרֵי תִיפְלוּת וְכֵן בִּסְעוּדָּתוֹ שֶׁל אוֹתוֹ רָשָׁע הַלָּלוּ אוֹמְרִים מָדִיּוֹת נָאוֹת וְהַלָּלוּ אוֹמְרִים פַּרְסִיּוֹת נָאוֹת אָמַר לָהֶם אֲחַשְׁוֵרוֹשׁ כְּלִי שֶׁאֲנִי מִשְׁתַּמֵּשׁ בּוֹ אֵינוֹ לֹא מָדִיִּי וְלֹא פַרְסִי אֶלָּא כַּשְׂדִּיִּי רְצוֹנְכֶם לִרְאוֹתָהּ אָמְרוּ לוֹ אִין וּבִלְבַד שֶׁתְּהֵא עֲרוּמָּה שֶׁבַּמִּדָּה שֶׁאָדָם מוֹדֵד בָּהּ מוֹדְדִין לוֹ מְלַמֵּד שֶׁהָיְתָה וַשְׁתִּי הָרְשָׁעָה מְבִיאָה בְּנוֹת יִשְׂרָאֵל עֲרוּמּוֹת וְעוֹשָׂה בָּהֶן מְלָאכָה בְּשַׁבָּת הַיְינוּ דִכְתִיב אַחַר הַדְּבָרִים הָאֵלֶּה כְּשׁוֹךְ חֲמַת הַמֶּלֶךְ אֲחַשְׁוֵרוֹשׁ זָכַר אֶת וַשְׁתִּי וְאֵת אֲשֶׁר עָשָׂתָה וְאֵת אֲשֶׁר נִגְזַר עָלֶיהָ כְּשֵׁם שֶׁעָשְׂתָה כָּךְ נִגְזַר עָלֶיהָ.

"On the seventh day, when the king's heart was gladdened with wine [he asked that Vashti be brought before him]." Until now, was his heart not gladdened with wine? Rava says: The seventh day refers to Shabbos. On that day, when Jews eat and drink, they begin with divrei Torah and words of praise; whereas when idolaters eat and drink, they begin with licentious talk. And so it was in the feast of that wicked man, there were those who were saying, "Median women are the most beautiful," and others who were saying, "Persian women are the most beautiful." Achashveirosh replied, "The utensil that I use is neither Median nor Persian, but Chaldean. Would you like to see it?" They said to him, "Yes, as long as she is unattired." For the same way a person measures, so are they measured, which teaches that wicked Vashti would bring Jewish girls, strip them down, and make them work on Shabbos. That is the meaning of the verse, "After these matters, as the king's anger subsided, he remembered Vashti and what she had done and that which was decreed upon her." Just as she did so was decreed upon her.

Why does the *Megillah* specify which day of the feast the conversation took place? Rava teaches that the *Megillah's* focus is not so much on the day of the feast, but on the day of the week. In Hebrew, all the days of the week are known simply as a number: *Yom Rishon, Yom Sheini* (Day One, Day Two). That's true of all the weekdays. But then we light candles and it's not Day Seven that is ushered in. The seventh day has a special name: Shabbos.

In many other languages, days of the week are associated with heavenly constellations. Sunday (named for the sun), Monday (named for the moon), Saturday (named for Saturn). Each day is dictated by the forces of nature and the seventh day is no different. Even if it is slightly different, it's no more spiritual than any other day of the week. On the contrary, Saturday is the day you can kick off your shoes and indulge in life's pleasures.

That's not Shabbos. As Rava emphasizes, the focus of Shabbos shouldn't be our physical indulgence. Our Shabbos tables should be filled with *divrei Torah* and *zemiros*. That doesn't mean we need to skimp on our Shabbos food and drink offerings. Rava specifically frames his teaching in the form "when Jews eat and drink, they begin with *divrei Torah* and words of praise [to Hashem]." He's not asking us to give up our food and drink. He just wants to make sure we know why we're enjoying our Shabbos delights. The herring, the gefilte fish, the cholent, and the kugel are all there to inspire us to greater spiritual intensity—not to mention the aged single malt.

Eating good food on Shabbos fulfills the mitzvah of *oneg Shabbos*. In fact, on Shabbos, we're endowed with a *neshamah yeseirah*—an additional soul. And despite its spiritual nature, our Sages teach that it enjoys a nice *kiddush*.[1] The key to remember is that the *kiddush* is only the facilitator. If we really want to feed our *neshamah yeseirah*, once we've enjoyed our physical Shabbos delights, we should then proceed to our spiritual delights.

Many of us are blessed with children who bring home from school a *d'var Torah* for the Shabbos table. When you first do it, it feels a little weird making the guests listen to your seven-year-old read off her *parashah* sheet for five minutes, but, after a few times, you realize how inspired they become, watching this kid's passion for Torah.

It shouldn't need to be said, but it's important to give the kids your undivided attention as they read their piece and engage with them on it. Let them know that this is the primary domain of your life. It's okay for them to know that you enjoy a nice vintage non-*mevushal* Cab Sauv. But they need to know that more important than the glass of wine is the *d'var Torah*. And of course, beyond the school piece, nowadays, there are a number of wonderful books available with plenty of stimuli for the Shabbos table.

In our home, we have a few favorites. There's *Torahific!* by Rabbi Maimon Elbaz. Each week he asks questions about the *parashah* and then provides kid-friendly answers from our great commentators across the millennia. And we love the questions and answers based on

---

1   *Rashi to Beitzah 16a.*

the responsa of Rav Yitzchak Zilberstein in the *What If?* and *Veha'arev Na* series.

When I was a young assistant rabbi in Long Beach, New York, I used to stay over with a lovely older couple. Friday nights would just be the three of us for an intimate dinner, but it was one of the highlights of my week. Each Erev Shabbos, the husband would go online and learn a new *zemer* tune. Some of the *zemiros* he sang were the regular old favorites, but with less famous tunes. The most exciting *zemiros*, however, were the ones in the book that nobody sings because most of us don't know any tunes for them. Here's the thing: the tunes exist and they're pretty catchy. Check them out online, learn them, and then, next Shabbos, take a few minutes to teach them to your kids and guests!

Shabbos is not just family Friday night dinner or Saturday lunch. We need to make an effort to make Shabbos be Shabbos. You will be inspired. Your kids will be inspired. Your guests will be inspired. May you always look forward to your radically different seventh day and may that Shabbos carry you and your family through the six mundane days of the week!

You Are Destined for Greatness

When Yaakov met Rachel, he proposed almost immediately.

She agreed, but then cautioned her fiancé, "My father, Lavan, is a swindler, and you will not be able to outwit him."

"What do you mean?" he asked.

"I have a sister, Leah, who is older than me," she replied, "and he will not marry me off before her."

But Yaakov was not fazed. He devised a system of sign language so that they would be able to ensure it was Rachel under the *chuppah*.

But as the big day approached, Rachel began to realize that her worst fears would soon materialize. As she'd assumed, her father was preparing Leah for the wedding. Unable to bear the thought of her sister's public embarrassment, she taught her the signs that Yaakov would be expecting…

בִּשְׂכַר צְנִיעוּת שֶׁהָיְתָה בָּהּ בְּרָחֵל זָכְתָה וְיָצָא מִמֶּנָּה שָׁאוּל וּבִשְׂכַר צְנִיעוּת שֶׁהָיָה בּוֹ בְּשָׁאוּל זָכָה וְיָצְאת מִמֶּנּוּ אֶסְתֵּר וּמַאי צְנִיעוּת הָיְתָה בָּהּ בְּרָחֵל דִּכְתִיב וַיַּגֵּד יַעֲקֹב לְרָחֵל כִּי אֲחִי אָבִיהָ הוּא וְכִי אֲחִי אָבִיהָ הוּא וַהֲלֹא בֶּן אֲחוֹת אָבִיהָ הוּא אֶלָּא אֲמַר לַהּ מִינַּסְבָּא לִי אֲמַרָה לֵיהּ אִין מִיהוּ אַבָּא רַמָּאָה הוּא וְלָא יָכְלַתְּ לֵיהּ אֲמַר לַהּ אָחִיו אֲנָא בְּרַמָּאוּת אֲמַרָה לֵיהּ וּמִי שָׁרֵי לְצַדִּיקֵי לְסַגּוּיֵי בְּרַמָּיוּתָא אֲמַר לַהּ אִין עִם נָבָר תִּתְבָּרַר וְעִם עִקֵּשׁ תִּתְפַּל אֲמַר לַהּ וּמַאי רַמָּיוּתָא אֲמַרָה לֵיהּ אִית לִי אֲחָתָא דְּקַשִּׁישָׁא מִינַּאי וְלָא מַנְסֵיב לִי מִקַּמַּהּ מָסַר לַהּ סִימָנִים כִּי מְטָא לֵילְיָא אֲמַרָה הַשְׁתָּא מִיכַּסְפָא אֲחָתַאי מַסְרַתִּינְהוּ נִיהֲלַהּ וְהַיְינוּ דִּכְתִיב וַיְהִי בַבֹּקֶר וְהִנֵּה הִיא לֵאָה מִכְּלָל דְּעַד הַשְׁתָּא

45

לָאו לֵאָה הִיא אֶלָּא מִתּוֹךְ סִימָנִין שֶׁמָּסְרָה רָחֵל לְלֵאָה לָא הֲוָה יָדַע עַד
הַשְׁתָּא לְפִיכָךְ זָכְתָה וְיָצָא מִמֶּנָּה שָׁאוּל וּמַה צְנִיעוּת הָיְתָה בְּשָׁאוּל דִּכְתִיב
וְאֶת דְּבַר הַמְּלוּכָה לֹא הִגִּיד לוֹ אֲשֶׁר אָמַר שְׁמוּאֵל זָכָה וְיָצָאת מִמֶּנּוּ אֶסְתֵּר
וְאָמַר רַבִּי אֶלְעָזָר כְּשֶׁהַקָּדוֹשׁ בָּרוּךְ הוּא פּוֹסֵק גְּדוּלָּה לְאָדָם פּוֹסֵק לְבָנָיו וְלִבְנֵי
בָנָיו עַד סוֹף כָּל הַדּוֹרוֹת שֶׁנֶּאֱמַר וַיּוֹשִׁיבֵם לָנֶצַח וַיִּגְבָּהוּ.

*In reward for the modesty shown by Rachel she merited that
Shaul should descend from her, and in reward for the modesty
shown by Shaul, he merited that Esther should descend from
him. What was the modesty shown by Rachel? As it is written,
"And Yaakov told Rachel that he was her father's brother."
Was he her father's brother? Wasn't he the son of her father's
sister? Rather, he said to her, "Will you marry me?" She said to
him, "Yes, but my father is a swindler..." When the wedding
night arrived, Rachel said to herself, "Now my sister will be
embarrassed." So she gave the signs to her. And this is as it is
written, "And it came to pass, that in the morning, behold, it
was Leah." Does this imply by inference that until now she was
not Leah? Rather, due to the distinguishing signs that Rachel
had given to Leah, he did not know this until now. Therefore,
Rachel merited that Shaul should descend from her. And what
was the modesty shown by Shaul? As it is written, "But of
the matter of the kingdom, of which Shmuel spoke, he did not
tell him." He merited that Esther would descend from him.
Rabbi Elazar said: When the Holy One, blessed be He, assigns
greatness to a person, He assigns it to his sons and to his son's
sons for all generations, as it is stated: "He establishes them
forever, and they are exalted."*

Rabbi Eliezer's statement is powerful. If the Almighty blesses you
with greatness, you will pass on that greatness to your children and
through the generations. When you act in an extraordinary fashion, as
Rachel and Shaul did, Hashem will imbue you with a spirit of greatness
that will last an eternity.

When you think about it, it cuts both ways. On the one hand, you
have so much riding on your efforts today. Not only will you impact

your own life, but the lives of your children and grandchildren will be forever changed by the decisions you make. If you act in an extraordinary manner, going above and beyond the call of duty, you will earn the mantle of greatness for generations.

On the other hand, the greatness you are enjoying today may be the result of extraordinary efforts made by your great-great-grandparents. It is their merit that is giving you strength today to be the incredible person you are on the road to becoming. That's a huge responsibility. They worked hard to draw down God's blessing into their family. But, of course, the blessing doesn't guarantee greatness. If you fail to make the necessary investment of time and energy, all their efforts will be for naught. When you do invest and exert yourself, however, you will be propelled to greatness, far beyond the level your own efforts might have accomplished.

Picture yourself playing on the football pitch. The game isn't going so well and it looks like it's game over, and not in your favor. Suddenly, you hear a resounding rallying cry of support. You turn around. Sitting in the bleachers are your parents, grandparents, and great-grandparents. They're cheering you on. They have faith in you. At that moment, you realize that you're not just playing for yourself; all these people are counting on you. There's a lot more riding on this than you first thought. You feel a renewed surge of energy and power, as you are propelled by the fans screaming your name.

You're not in this life alone. You have generations of forebears cheering you on and rooting for your success. They're rooting for you, because they are your roots. They have skin in the game, because you are their flesh and blood. Your success is their success. When you are victorious, everything they invested, everything they sacrificed throughout their lifetimes, becomes worth it. They have faith in you and are betting on your success.

When the Maggid of Mezeritch was a little boy, the family home burned down. *Baruch Hashem*, the family was able to escape the inferno unscathed. Standing outside the house, as they watched everything go up in flames, young Dov Ber's mother began to cry.

"Mama, why are you crying? It's only *gashmiyus*. Material possessions are not something to shed tears over."

"My dear Berel'e," she replied, "I am not crying over the *gashmiyus*. You're right, that's all meaningless. I am upset because our family tree, describing your special *yichus*—all your amazing forebears—has been destroyed."

"Mama, don't cry," replied little Dov Ber. "Our family's *yichus* will start anew, beginning with me."

You are destined for greatness based on the merits of your forebears. Don't let them down. But, even more importantly, the greatness of your future descendants is riding on your efforts today. May you always do your very best for your great team!

The Bible Is a Jewish Book

Amram, the father of Moshe, was the leader of his generation. When he heard that the wicked Pharaoh said, "Every son that is born you shall cast into the river, and every daughter you shall keep alive," he said, "We are laboring for nothing by bringing children into the world to be killed." And so, he arose and divorced his wife. All others who saw this followed his example and arose and divorced their wives. His daughter, Miriam, said to him, "Father, your decree is harsher for the Jewish people than that of Pharaoh, as Pharaoh decreed only with regard to the males, but you decreed both on the males and on the females. And now, no children will be born. Additionally, Pharaoh decreed to kill them only in this world, but you decreed in this world and in the World to Come, as those not born will not enter the World to Come. Additionally, concerning Pharaoh the wicked, it is uncertain whether his decree will be fulfilled or not. You are a righteous person, and as such, your decrees will certainly be fulfilled, as it is stated with regard to the righteous, 'You shall also decree a thing, and it shall be established unto you.'" Amram accepted his daughter's words, arose, and remarried his wife, and all those who saw this followed his example and arose and remarried their wives.

Miriam then prophesied, "My mother is destined to bear a son who will redeem the Jewish people from Egypt." Sure enough, when Moshe was born the entire house was filled with light, and Amram stood up

49

and kissed Miriam on the head, and said to her, "My daughter, your prophecy has been fulfilled." But after concealing his birth for three months, they could no longer hide him. Moshe was sent down the Nile river in a basket and Amram arose and snapped at his daughter, "My daughter, where is your prophecy now?" But Miriam did not give up her faith. "She stood at a distance to know" what would be with the end of her prophecy. Finally, after the Children of Israel had passed through the Red Sea on dry land, the Torah calls Miriam "the prophetess," because at that moment, it became clear to all that her words as a young child had indeed come to pass.

וַיָּסַר הַמֶּלֶךְ אֶת טַבַּעְתּוֹ אָמַר רַבִּי אַבָּא בַּר כָּהֲנָא גְּדוֹלָה הֲסָרַת טַבַּעַת יוֹתֵר מֵאַרְבָּעִים וּשְׁמוֹנָה נְבִיאִים וְשֶׁבַע נְבִיאוֹת שֶׁנִּתְנַבְּאוּ לָהֶן לְיִשְׂרָאֵל שֶׁכּוּלָּן לֹא הֶחֱזִירוּם לְמוּטָב וְאִילּוּ הֲסָרַת טַבַּעַת הֶחֱזִירָתַן לְמוּטָב תָּנוּ רַבָּנַן אַרְבָּעִים וּשְׁמוֹנָה נְבִיאִים וְשֶׁבַע נְבִיאוֹת נִתְנַבְּאוּ לָהֶם לְיִשְׂרָאֵל וְלֹא פִּחֲתוּ וְלֹא הוֹתִירוּ עַל מַה שֶׁכָּתוּב בַּתּוֹרָה חוּץ מִמִּקְרָא מְגִילָּה מַאי דְּרוּשׁ אָמַר רַבִּי חִיָּיא בַּר אָבִין אָמַר רַבִּי יְהוֹשֻׁעַ בֶּן קָרְחָה וּמָה מֵעַבְדוּת לְחֵירוּת אָמְרִינַן שִׁירָה מִמִּיתָה לְחַיִּים לֹא כָּל שֶׁכֵּן וְתוּ לֵיכָּא וְהָכְתִיב וַיְהִי אִישׁ אֶחָד מִן הָרָמָתַיִם צוֹפִים אֶחָד מִמָּאתַיִם צוֹפִים שֶׁנִּתְנַבְּאוּ לָהֶם לְיִשְׂרָאֵל מִיהְוֶה טוּבָא הֲווֹ כִּדְתַנְיָא הַרְבֵּה נְבִיאִים עָמְדוּ לָהֶם לְיִשְׂרָאֵל כִּפְלַיִם כְּיוֹצְאֵי מִצְרַיִם אֶלָּא נְבוּאָה שֶׁהוּצְרְכָה לְדוֹרוֹת נִכְתְּבָה וְשֶׁלֹּא הוּצְרְכָה לֹא נִכְתְּבָה שֶׁבַע נְבִיאוֹת מַאן נִינְהוּ שָׂרָה מִרְיָם דְּבוֹרָה חַנָּה אֲבִיגַיִל חוּלְדָּה וְאֶסְתֵּר שָׂרָה דִּכְתִיב אֲבִי מִלְכָּה וַאֲבִי יִסְכָּה וְאָמַר רַבִּי יִצְחָק יִסְכָּה זוֹ שָׂרָה וְלָמָּה נִקְרָא שְׁמָהּ יִסְכָּה שֶׁסָּכְתָה בְּרוּחַ הַקֹּדֶשׁ שֶׁנֶּאֱמַר כֹּל אֲשֶׁר תֹּאמַר אֵלֶיךָ שָׂרָה שְׁמַע בְּקוֹלָהּ דָּבָר אַחֵר יִסְכָּה שֶׁהַכֹּל סוֹכִין בְּיוֹפְיָהּ מִרְיָם דִּכְתִיב וַתִּקַּח מִרְיָם הַנְּבִיאָה אֲחוֹת אַהֲרֹן וְלֹא אֲחוֹת מֹשֶׁה אָמַר רַב נַחְמָן אָמַר רַב שֶׁהָיְתָה מִתְנַבְּאָה כְּשֶׁהִיא אֲחוֹת אַהֲרֹן וְאוֹמֶרֶת עֲתִידָה אִמִּי שֶׁתֵּלֵד בֵּן שֶׁיּוֹשִׁיעַ אֶת יִשְׂרָאֵל וּבְשָׁעָה שֶׁנּוֹלַד נִתְמַלֵּא כָּל הַבַּיִת כּוּלּוֹ אוֹרָה עָמַד אָבִיהָ וּנְשָׁקָהּ עַל רֹאשָׁהּ אָמַר לָהּ בִּתִּי נִתְקַיְּימָה נְבוּאָתֵיךְ וְכֵיוָן שֶׁהִשְׁלִיכוּהוּ לַיְאוֹר עָמַד אָבִיהָ וּטְפָחָהּ עַל רֹאשָׁהּ וְאָמַר לָהּ בִּתִּי הֵיכָן נְבוּאָתֵיךְ הַיְינוּ דִּכְתִיב וַתֵּתַצַּב אֲחוֹתוֹ מֵרָחוֹק לְדֵעָה מָה יְהֵא בְּסוֹף נְבוּאָתָהּ.

"The king removed his signet ring from his hand and he gave it to Haman." Rabbi Aba bar Kahana taught: The removal of this ring was more powerful than the forty-eight prophets and seven prophetesses who prophesied to Israel, none of whom

were able to return them to righteousness; whereas the removal of the ring returned them to righteousness. The Rabbis taught: Forty-eight prophets and seven prophetesses prophesied to Israel and did not detract from nor add to that which is written in the Torah, except for the reading of the Megillah. How did they expound this obligation? Rabbi Chiya bar Avin quoted Rabbi Yehoshua ben Korcha who explains: If we sang a song at the Red Sea when we were taken from slavery to freedom, should we not offer praise for being taken from death to life? Were there no more than forty-eight prophets and seven prophetesses? Is it not written in the Book of Shmuel, "There was one man from Ramasayim-Tzofim," which is interpreted to mean "one of the two hundred (maasayim) seers (tzofim) who prophesied to Israel"? There were indeed many more prophets, as the Beraisa teaches: Many prophets arose among Israel, double the number of those who left Egypt. However, the prophecy that was needed for all future generations was recorded in Scripture, and that which was unnecessary was not recorded...Who were the seven prophetesses? Sarah, Miriam, Devorah, Chanah, Avigayil, Chuldah, and Esther. Sarah, as it is written, "The father of Milkah, and the father of Yiskah." And Rabbi Yitzchak said: Yiskah is Sarah. And why was she called Yiskah? For she saw (sachsah) by means of Divine inspiration, as it is stated, "In all that Sarah has said to you, hearken to her voice." Alternatively, Yiskah, for all gazed (sochin) upon her beauty. Miriam, as it is written, "And Miriam the prophetess, the sister of Aharon, took a tambourine in her hand." And was she not the sister of Moshe? Rav Nachman said that Rav said: For she prophesied when she was the sister of Aharon, and she would say: My mother is destined to bear a son... "And his sister stood at a distance to know," i.e., to know what would be with the end of her prophecy.

While most of us are familiar with the story of Miriam, how many of us are able to retell the story of Chuldah? How many of us are able to list the forty-eight prophets? Just in case we're tempted to dismiss the stories as minor and insignificant, the Gemara informs us of the difference between these specific fifty-five prophets and prophetesses and all of the myriad Biblical-era prophets. These prophecies are relevant for all time, not just the period in history when they occurred.

I was once sitting on a plane when I overheard two girls behind me discussing the Bible. One asked the other if she'd read the "Good Book." The other responded that she had indeed read it a number of times. The first one was impressed because she was only two thirds of the way through her reading of the Old Testament. When I heard that, I was overwhelmed with feelings of humility. Here are these two young ladies who were familiar with most of our Tanach, and I, a rabbi, hadn't made my way through even once! I immediately resolved to start learning Tanach on a regular basis.

The reason many of us are not conversant in the Bible is that we read through it, and we find it arcane and complex, and we perceive it to have been written to an audience thousands of years ago. We read the prophecies of Yirmiyahu and we think he was talking to the Jews prior to the destruction of the First Temple. We read the Book of *Ezra* and we think it's a story of the return from Babylonia, something that happened long ago, sometime in the distant past.

But the Gemara teaches that any prophecy that is recorded in Tanach is "needed for all future generations"! The challenge for us is to read the Tanach with enough depth and concentration, together with our classic commentators, to develop insights that enable us to apply the prophets' messages to our lives today. Torah comes from the word *horaah*, meaning instruction or lesson. The Torah is not a storybook; it is an instruction manual for how we are to live. The *Torah She'bichsav*, the Written Torah, consists not just of the Chumash, but of the entire Tanach—the Torah, *Neviim*, and *Kesuvim*. It's all relevant; the lessons and instructions throughout Tanach were recorded for posterity because they contain an important message for all generations. But if you rarely read and familiarize yourself with the Tanach, it's impossible to hear the message.

It's time to start learning Tanach. Start by taking an English copy and devoting ten minutes a day to simply reading through it. You will finish it in less than a year. Next year, read some of it each day in the Hebrew. After that you can add commentaries to ensure you are getting the accurate meaning. But, most importantly, after you've read it, may you be inspired to think about the message of the prophecy you've read and how it is relevant to your life today!

You Have the Power to Give Berachos

Despite the Torah's stern caution against counting the Children of Israel, King David decided to take a census of the people. Realizing his error, he cried to Hashem, "I have sinned grievously in what I have done. Please, Hashem, forgive the guilt of Your servant, for I have acted foolishly." When David arose in the morning, the word of Hashem came to the prophet Gad, "Go and tell David, 'Thus said the Lord: I hold three things over you; choose one of them, and I will bring it upon you.'"

Gad came to David and asked him, "Shall a seven-year famine come upon you in the land, or shall you be in flight from your adversaries for three months while they pursue you, or shall there be three days of pestilence in your land? Now consider carefully what reply I shall take back to Him who sent me." David said to Gad, "I am in great distress. Let us fall into the hands of Hashem, for His compassion is great; and let me not fall into the hands of men." So Hashem sent a pestilence upon Israel from morning until the set time; and seventy thousand of the people died.

But when the angel turned his hand against Jerusalem to destroy it, Hashem renounced further punishment and said to the angel who was destroying the people, "Enough! Stay your hand!" The angel of Hashem was then by the threshing floor of Aravnah the Jebusite. When David saw the angel who was striking down the people, he said to Hashem, "I alone am guilty, I alone have done wrong; but these poor sheep, what have they done? Let Your hand fall upon me and my father's house!"

Gad came to David the same day and said to him, "Go and set up an altar to Hashem on the threshing floor of Aravnah the Jebusite." David went up, following Gad's instructions, as Hashem had commanded. Aravnah looked out and saw the king and his courtiers approaching him. So Aravnah went out and bowed low to the king, with his face to the ground. And Aravnah asked, "Why has my lord, the king, come to his servant?" David replied, "To buy the threshing floor from you, that I may build an altar to Hashem, and that the plague against the people may stop." Aravnah said to David, "Let my lord, the king, take it and offer up whatever he sees fit. Here are oxen for a burnt offering, and the threshing boards and the gear of the oxen for wood. All this, O king, Aravnah gives to Your Majesty. And may Hashem your God respond to you with favor!"

But the king replied to Aravnah, "No, I will buy them from you at a price. I cannot sacrifice to Hashem, my God, burnt offerings that have cost me nothing." So David bought the threshing floor and the oxen for fifty shekels of silver. And David built there an altar to Hashem and sacrificed burnt offerings and offerings of well-being. Hashem responded to the plea for the land, and the plague against Israel stopped.

וְאָמַר רַבִּי אֶלְעָזָר אָמַר רַבִּי חֲנִינָא לְעוֹלָם אַל תְּהִי בִּרְכַּת הֶדְיוֹט קַלָּה
בְּעֵינֶיךָ שֶׁהֲרֵי שְׁנֵי גְדוֹלֵי הַדּוֹר בֵּרְכוּם שְׁנֵי הֶדְיוֹטוֹת וְנִתְקַיְּימָה בָּהֶן וְאֵלּוּ הֵן
דָּוִד וְדָנִיֵּאל דָּוִד דִּבְרָכֵיהּ אֲרַוְנָה דִּכְתִיב וַיֹּאמֶר אֲרַוְנָה אֶל הַמֶּלֶךְ וְגוֹ׳ דָּנִיֵּאל
דִּבְרָכֵיהּ דָּרְיָוֶשׁ דִּכְתִיב אֱלָקָךְ דִּי אַנְתְּ פָּלַח לֵיהּ בִּתְדִירָא הוּא יְשֵׁיזְבִינָךְ
וְאָמַר רַבִּי אֶלְעָזָר אָמַר רַבִּי חֲנִינָא אַל תְּהִי קִלְלַת הֶדְיוֹט קַלָּה בְּעֵינֶיךָ שֶׁהֲרֵי
אֲבִימֶלֶךְ קִלֵּל אֶת שָׂרָה הִנֵּה הוּא לָךְ כְּסוּת עֵינַיִם וְנִתְקַיֵּים בְּזַרְעָהּ וַיְהִי כִּי זָקֵן
יִצְחָק וַתִּכְהֶיןָ עֵינָיו.

Rabbi Elazar quoted Rabbi Chanina: Let not the blessing of an ordinary man be light in your eyes, for two men great in their generation received blessings from ordinary men which were fulfilled in them. They were David and Daniel. David was

> *blessed by Aravnah, as it is written, "And Aravnah said to the*
> *king..." Daniel was blessed by Darius, as it is written, "Your*
> *God whom you serve continually, He will deliver you." And*
> *Rabbi Elazar quoted Rabbi Chanina: Let not the curse of an*
> *ordinary man be light in your eyes, because Avimelech cursed*
> *Sarah, saying, "Behold he is to you a covering of the eyes." This*
> *was fulfilled in her offspring, "And it came to pass that when*
> *Yitzchak grew old his eyes became dim."*

Jew or non-Jew, the Gemara teaches that blessings and curses are real
and have a tangible effect. The *Seforno* explains that our ability to bless
derives from each human being having been created in the image of
God.[1] When man was created, the Torah says, "And Adam became a living soul."[2] *Onkelos* translates the verse, "And Adam became a speaking
spirit," meaning that the distinction of humankind lies in our ability
to speak. Speech represents our connection between body and soul.[3]
When we channel that immense power, we can move worlds.

Sometimes we think that we are not worthy of giving blessings. Only
big rebbes, *roshei yeshiva*, or *mekubalim* have the power of *berachah*.
That's not the case, says Rabbi Elazar. Even the most ordinary of people
have a profound ability to impact the welfare of another by their words.
Every Friday night we bless our children. But it's not only your biologi-
cal children that you are able to bless. They're the model and example of
your power to give *berachos*. Anyone you confer blessing upon becomes
your "child," another human being for whom you have given birth to
positivity in his life.

While it is scary to think about the Gemara's warning that even
the curses of someone you consider a "nobody" should not be taken
lightly, the Jewish people have a special protection. Hashem bestowed
a Heavenly gift upon our forefather Avraham, which he bequeathed to
his children throughout the generations. "Those who bless you, I shall

---

1   *Bereishis* 32:1.
2   Ibid., 2:7.
3   Gevhard, *Shiurim*, p. 101.

bless. And those who curse you I shall curse."[4] While blessings and curses are impactful, they are likewise reflected back onto the individual who cast them. The good side of that equation is that the more blessings you give, the more you will receive.

Blessings and curses may take the form of *"baruch"* and *"arur,"* but they needn't necessarily be phrased so explicitly. Sometimes we say things that bring about blessing in another person's life. And other times, God forbid, the words we use are motivated by improper intent. When you build people up with your words, you endow them with blessing. When you put others down with your words, it is like you are cursing them.

And sometimes, even when we think we are blessing people by offering them constructive criticism, we need to make sure the recipient will be able to accept the "blessing." In *Mishlei*, Shlomo HaMelech cautions, "He who corrects a scorner brings shame upon himself and he who reproves a wicked man acquires his blemish. Do not reprove a scorner, lest he hate you; reprove a wise man and he will love you."[5] If there's any chance whatsoever that your words will come back to bite you, then it's probably best not to say anything.

Your faculty of speech has extraordinary power. Use it as frequently as possible to bless people by building them up. Every interaction should be one of blessing. May everyone know you as a person who brings light and joy into their lives, the individual with whom every encounter is one where people walk away feeling uplifted and inspired!

---

4   *Bereishis* 12:3.
5   *Mishlei* 9:7.

Your Life Could Go Either Way

A chashveirosh is tossing and turning in bed, unable to fall asleep. After reading his diary, he realizes he never rewarded Mordechai for saving his life. Just then, Haman arrives and the king asks him how he should honor the fellow he holds dear. Thinking Achashveirosh is referring to him, he suggests that the honoree be adorned in the king's robes and taken for a ride upon the royal horse. Achashveirosh agrees and instructs Haman to make it happen for Mordechai. Downtrodden, off Haman goes to find his nemesis.

He offers the clothes to Mordechai, but he doesn't accept them. "I'm sorry," says Mordechai, "It's not right to don the royal robes until I've been to the bathhouse and taken a haircut." Meanwhile, Esther has all the bathhouses and barbershops closed. So Haman has to take Mordechai into the bathhouse and attend to him personally. He washes him, and then begins to cut his hair. Suddenly, he lets out a deep groan. Startled, Mordechai asks him, "What happened?"

אָמַר לֵיהּ קוּם לְבוּשׁ הָנֵי מָאנֵי וּרְכוֹב הַאי סוּסְיָא דְּבָעֵי לָךְ מַלְכָּא אָמַר לֵיהּ לָא יָכֵילְנָא עַד דְּעָיֵילְנָא לְבֵי בָנֵי וְאֶשְׁקוֹל לְמַזְיָיא דְּלָאו אוֹרַח אַרְעָא לְאִשְׁתַּמּוֹשֵׁי בְּמָאנֵי דְּמַלְכָּא הָכִי שַׁדְּרָה אֶסְתֵּר וְאֲסַרְתִּינְהוּ לְכוּלְהוּ בֵּי בָנֵי וּלְכוּלְהוּ אוּמָּנֵי עַיֵּילֵיהּ אִיהוּ לְבֵי בָנֵי וְאַסְחֵיהּ וְאֲזַל וְאַיְיתִי זוּזָא מִבֵּיתֵיהּ וְקָא שָׁקֵיל בֵּיהּ מַזְיֵיהּ בַּהֲדֵי דְּקָא שָׁקֵיל לֵיהּ אִיגְּנַח וְאִיתְּנַח אָמַר לֵיהּ אַמַּאי קָא מִיתְּנַחַתְּ אָמַר לֵיהּ גַּבְרָא דַּהֲוָה חָשִׁיב לֵיהּ לְמַלְכָּא מִכּוּלְּהוּ רַבְרְבָנוֹהִי הַשְׁתָּא לִישַׁוְּויֵהּ בַּלָּנָאֵי וְסַפָּר אָמַר לֵיהּ רָשָׁע וְלָאו סַפָּר שֶׁל כְּפַר קַרְצוּם הָיֵית תָּנָא

הָמָן סַפָּר שֶׁל כְּפַר קַרְצוּם הָיָה עֶשְׂרִים וּשְׁתַּיִם שָׁנָה בָּתַר דְּשַׁקְלִינְהוּ לְמַזְיֵיהּ
לְבִשִׁינְהוּ לְמָאנֵיהּ.

Haman said to Mordechai, "Arise and don these garments and
ride on this horse, for the king wants you to do so." Mordechai
said to him, "I cannot do so until I enter the bathhouse and
trim my hair..." He said to him, "Why do you groan?" Haman
said to him, "The man whom the king had once regarded above
all his other ministers is now made a bathhouse attendant
and a barber." Mordechai said to him, "Wicked man, were
you not once the barber of the village of Kartzum?" It was
taught: Haman was the barber of the village of Kartzum for
twenty-two years. After Haman trimmed his hair, he dressed
Mordechai in the royal garments.

What is the meaning of this strange exchange between Mordechai
and Haman? Why do we need to know that Haman used to work as
a hairdresser? Clearly, there's more to this Gemara than the opportunity to ridicule the villain of the Purim story.

Rav Kalonymus HaZaken[1] quotes the Gemara in *Shabbos* (156a) that
"an individual born during the Mars hour will be a spiller of blood. Says
Rav Ashi: Thus, he is destined to become a blood-letter, a highwayman,
a *shochet*, or a mohel."

Likewise, explains Rav Kalonymus, one might use one's skills
with a pair of scissors to become a barber or to become a murderer.
Mordechai's exhortation to Haman, calling him "wicked" was not
a taunt, but a directive to *teshuvah*. Here was his opportunity to repent
from his murderous intentions and return to his earlier calling. Instead
of trying to destroy the world that is built upon the twenty-two letters
of the Hebrew alphabet, he should have been using his talents for constructive purposes, as he did for twenty-two years earlier in his life.[2]

Every person in this world has a distinct and special mission to fulfill.
If we were all of the same mind and ability, not only would life be rather

1   Cited in *Ein Yaakov (Masores Hashas), Likkutim*, p. 228.
2   *Orach Yesharim*, Rabbi M.Z. Taksin.

boring, but we would not be able to survive in this world. Everyone would choose the same job and business opportunity. Instead, Hashem has created all of us different. Each of us is blessed with certain character traits and a unique skill set.

But that doesn't presume our outcomes. Whatever talents and tendencies we have are merely the starting point with multiple directions open and available to us. The individual who is handy with a knife could become Don Corleone, or he could become a world-class surgeon. The computer whiz could become a cyber hacker, able to break into and steal from the most secure websites, or he could become a famous programmer, writing coding systems that are life changing.

Hashem has blessed you with unbelievable abilities and talents. Just as there is nobody else in the world with the same unique DNA genome as you, there is no other person with the exact same calling and character. You have a role to fulfill in this world that cannot be fulfilled by any other person.

But the mere fact that you have that potential does not guarantee that you will indeed fulfill your mission. It's your choice how you use your talents. Will you utilize your Heavenly endowment for the betterment of humankind, or will you constantly seek to maximize your own pleasure and benefit in this world? Will you use your God-given talents for constructive purposes, or God forbid, for destructive purposes? Will your investments of time and energy be eternal, or will they be short-lived?

You are one of a kind. The Almighty has created a unique human being with a unique character and calling. But now the ball's in your court. May you reach your greatest potential and fulfill your unique mission on Earth!

Align Yourself with Heaven

A prince was once taken captive by enemy troops while still a young boy. Taken far away from the kingdom, he grew up in a foreign land, speaking a different language and practicing different customs to those of his parents' home. One day, he found out who he really was and became determined to make his way back to his birthplace and life of royal privilege.

"Aren't you worried you won't fit in?" his friends asked him.

"Of course not," the prince replied. "It might be strange at first, but it's my home, my heritage; it's where I belong."[1]

שִׁמְעוֹן הַפָּקוּלִי הִסְדִּיר שְׁמוֹנֶה עֶשְׂרֵה בְּרָכוֹת לִפְנֵי רַבָּן גַּמְלִיאֵל עַל הַסֵּדֶר
בְּיַבְנֶה אָמַר רַבִּי יוֹחָנָן וְאָמְרִי לַהּ בְּמַתְנִיתָא תָּנָא מֵאָה וְעֶשְׂרִים זְקֵנִים וּבָהֶם
כַּמָּה נְבִיאִים תִּיקְנוּ שְׁמוֹנֶה עֶשְׂרֵה בְּרָכוֹת עַל הַסֵּדֶר וּמַה רָאוּ לוֹמַר תְּשׁוּבָה
אַחַר בִּינָה דִּכְתִיב וּלְבָבוֹ יָבִין וָשָׁב וְרָפָא לוֹ אִי הָכִי לֵימָא רְפוּאָה בָּתְרַהּ
דִּתְשׁוּבָה לָא סָלְקָא דַּעְתָּךְ דִּכְתִיב וְיָשׁוֹב אֶל ה' וִירַחֲמֵהוּ וְאֶל אֱלֹקֵינוּ כִּי
יַרְבֶּה לִסְלוֹחַ וּמַאי חָזֵית דְּסָמְכַת אַהָא סְמוֹךְ אַהָא כְּתַב קְרָא אַחֲרִינָא
הַסּוֹלֵחַ לְכָל עֲוֹנֵיכִי הָרוֹפֵא לְכָל תַּחֲלוּאָיְכִי הַגּוֹאֵל מִשַּׁחַת חַיָּיְכִי לְמֵימְרָא
דִּגְאוּלָה וּרְפוּאָה בָּתַר סְלִיחָה הִיא וְהִכְתִיב וָשָׁב וְרָפָא לוֹ הַהוּא לָאו רְפוּאָה
דִּתַחְלוּאִים הִיא אֶלָּא רְפוּאָה דִּסְלִיחָה הִיא.

---

1   *Shemos Rabbah* 33:7.

> *Shimon HaPakuli arranged the eighteen blessings of the Amidah prayer before Rabban Gamliel in their order in Yavneh. Rabbi Yochanan said, and some say that it was taught in a Beraisa: A hundred and twenty Elders, and among them several prophets, established the eighteen blessings in their order. Why did they see fit to institute to say the blessing of repentance after the blessing of understanding? As it is written, "And they will understand with their heart, repent, and be healed." If so, let us say the blessing of healing after the blessing of repentance? This cannot enter your mind, as it is written, "And let him return to the Lord, and He will have compassion upon him; and to our God, for He will abundantly pardon." But what did you see to rely on this verse? Rely on the other. Another verse, in which it is written, "Who forgives all your iniquities, Who heals all your diseases, Who redeems your life from the pit." Is that to say that the blessings of redemption and healing should be placed following the blessing of forgiveness? But isn't it written, "Repent, and be healed"? That verse is referring not to the healing from illness, but rather to the healing of forgiveness.*

What's the difference between the *berachos* of repentance and forgiveness in the *Shemoneh Esreh*? If we're asking Hashem to return us, does that not then imply that He's forgiven us for our sins? Presumably it's a symbiotic relationship. We repent. He forgives. Why do we need two separate *berachos*?

In the first *berachah* in the sequence of the blessings of supplication, we beseech Heaven for understanding. We ask Hashem that He grant us the wisdom to successfully navigate the travails of life. Once that request has been granted, everything flows naturally from there. With the blessing of wisdom, we begin to understand that the best way to navigate life is to place ourselves in Hashem's hand. If we simply trust Him to guide us, we can rest assured that everything will be okay.

That perspective forms the foundation of the next blessing, asking Hashem to return us. Of course, He won't do the work of *teshuvah* for us. But we're asking Him to help us along the way and open the right doors so we don't give up as we strive to better our ways.

The key though, is to remember that *teshuvah* doesn't mean changing ourselves into something different. It means "returning" to the royal palace, the place where we originated. Just like the prince who was kidnapped as a young child, our Sages advise that the way to turn things around in our lives is to remember that we are reclaiming our birthrights. That's the meaning of, "The Torah that Moshe commanded us is an inheritance for the congregation of Yaakov."[2] It's our inheritance. It belongs to us. It's ours for the taking whenever we "come back" to claim it.[3]

So far in the *Amidah*, that return does not speak of our sins. It's simply an attitude shift that we're striving for. We're asking Hashem to help us align our thoughts and desires with the will of Heaven. That we learn to trust Him and know that whatever happens in our lives, He has a plan. The wisdom of this attitude leads to a new way of looking at life that allows a person to stop worrying, with the knowledge that everything that happens comes from Heaven.

Some people mistakenly believe that *teshuvah* is dependent upon receiving atonement for their prior mistakes. What then happens is that they get caught up in a state of inertia. Unable to fix everything, they either stall or give up entirely. In contrast, the wise person first returns to the ideal state of being, and only afterward starts working to clean up his past.

It's much easier to rectify old transgressions when you're in a new frame of mind, a frame that couldn't contemplate acting again today as you did yesterday. Rabbi Abraham J. Twerski offers an example from the *Ibn Ezra* about the sin of coveting your neighbor's property. How can the Torah command a person not to desire something when they can't help it? The answer is that one must understand that something belonging to another person is impossible to attain. Imagine you heard there were mountains of diamonds and gold on a star billions of miles

---

2   *Devarim* 33:4.
3   *Shemos Rabbah* 33:7.

away, free for the taking. Would you desire them? Not really. Because you know they're not reachable. That should be the attitude toward the property of another. It's simply unattainable because Hashem has destined it for someone else. When you return to the palace and align your mind with Hashem's plan, all sinful desire simply dissipates.[4]

That's why the prayer for forgiveness is completely separate from the prayer for *teshuvah*. Once you've aligned your will with God's will, He will assist with remedying any previous missteps. At that point you too will wonder why you ever acted as you did.

If you're looking to get back on spiritual track, don't let the *yetzer hara* convince you that you're not worthy until you clean up your act. Just refocus and become the person you know Hashem wants you to be. Start tuning in to the Divine will and things will start falling into place. As long as you set out each day knowing that Hashem is in control, all your worries will disappear. May you pray for wisdom, use that wisdom to refocus, and may all your prior errors be washed away!

---

4   *On Prayer*, p. 167.

Silence Is Golden

abbi Yosi HaGelili was on the way to Lod, when he realized he was going round and round in circles. Just then, he encountered Bruriah, the wife of Rabbi Meir.

"On which path do we walk to Lod?" he asked her.

"Foolish Galilean," she replied. "You should have asked more succinctly: Which to Lod?"[1]

דְּרַשׁ רַבִּי יְהוּדָה אִישׁ כְּפַר גְּבוֹרַיָּא וְאָמְרִי לַהּ אִישׁ כְּפַר גִּבּוֹר חַיִל מַאי דִּכְתִיב לְךָ דּוּמִיָּה תְהִלָּה סַמָּא דְּכוֹלָּה מַשְׁתּוּקָא כִּי אֲתָא רַב דִּימִי אֲמַר אָמְרִי בְּמַעַרְבָא מִלָּה בְּסֶלַע מַשְׁתּוּקָא בִּתְרֵין.

Rabbi Yehudah of Kfar Giboria, and some say he was from Kfar Gibor Chayil, taught: What is the meaning of that which is written, "For You, silence is praise"? The best remedy of all is silence. When Rav Dimi came, he said: In the West, they say: If a word is worth one sela, silence is worth two.

The *Orchos Tzaddikim* describes what makes silence so virtuous. Until one has spoken, he is the ruler over his words. Once a person has spoken, the words rule over him.[2] In this vein, the *Mivchar Hapeninim*

---

1   *Eruvin* 53b.
2   *Shaar Hashetikah,* cited in *Maseches Avos, Otzar Geonei Sefarad, Kedem, Otzeros* 1:84.

explains why silence is twice as valuable as speech.[3] Occasionally, you walk away from a conversation, regretting not having said something you should have mentioned. Far more often, however, you walk away from a conversation regretting having said too much. Rav Dimi's message is: When in doubt, err on the side of caution and keep quiet.

In *Pirkei Avos*, Rabbi Akiva teaches, "A fence for wisdom is silence."[4] The *Machzor Vitri* explains that when a person strives for silence, he will never rush to respond to a query without giving it due consideration. When he eventually answers, the response will shine with wisdom. Likewise, Rabbeinu Yonah relates the advice to the Mishnah in chapter 5 of *Pirkei Avos* that describes the attributes of the wise man. "He does not speak before someone greater than him in wisdom. He does not interrupt his friend. And about that which he hasn't heard, he says 'I haven't heard.'"

All of these attributes point to the value of silence. In contrast with the wise man, the big talker rushes to offer an opinion even when there are smarter people in the room. The big talker interrupts other people. The big talker thinks he's an expert on everything, even those matters he really doesn't know much about.

The Gemara in *Pesachim* teaches, "Silence is beautiful for the wise man. And most certainly for the fool."[5] Sometimes, it can be difficult at first to discern whether or not someone is wise. Sadly, many people don't leave others guessing very long. The second they open their mouths, it becomes clear. The secret to maintaining a reputation for wisdom is the less said, the better.

Nevertheless, our Sages do offer a cautionary caveat. When it comes to Torah matters, you can't keep quiet. Another famous teaching, in *Pirkei Avos*, informs us that "a shy person does not learn."[6] It's one thing to keep quiet and absorb the wisdom of your teachers. It's quite another if you fail to ask when you don't understand something.

---

3   Ibid.
4   *Avos* 3:13.
5   *Pesachim* 99a.
6   *Avos* 2:5.

In fact, after telling the story of her encounter with Rabbi Yosi HaGelili, the Gemara in *Eruvin* continues with a story that happened when Bruriah finds a student who is learning Torah quietly. She chastises him and tells him that one must learn Torah with every fiber of his being. The Gemara goes on to tell of Rabbi Eliezer's student who learned quietly and ended up forgetting all his learning.[7]

We've all heard the classic Miranda warning, "You have the right to remain silent. Anything you say may be used against you." In our tradition, this warning is not new. But it's not just about the less we say, the less we incriminate ourselves. It's that the less we say, the greater the opportunity to appear wise and gain wisdom from others as we tune in to the words of those with greater knowledge and understanding. The only exception to the rule is to remember to speak up when we don't understand. May you display wisdom and gain wisdom by mastering the art of silence!

---

7   *Eruvin* 54a.

Embrace the Stress of Life

F ollowing Eliyahu HaNavi's showdown and victory over the prophets of the Baal on Mount Carmel, Queen Izevel threatens to have him killed. Frightened, he flees into the wilderness. After walking for forty days and forty nights, he arrives at Sinai. He enters the cave Moshe Rabbeinu once occupied and spends the night there.

The word of Hashem then comes to him, "Why are you here, Eliyahu?"

"I have been zealous for Heaven," replies Eliyahu, "but the Israelites have forsaken Your covenant, torn down Your altars, and put Your prophets to the sword. I alone am left, and they are out to take my life."

Suddenly the Divine presence passes by. There is a great and mighty wind, splitting mountains and shattering rocks by the power of Hashem; but Hashem was not in the wind. After the wind came an earthquake; but Hashem was not in the earthquake. After the earthquake came a fire; but Hashem was not in the fire. And after the fire came a soft murmuring sound.

When Eliyahu hears it, he wraps his mantle about his face and goes outside, standing at the entrance of the cave. Once again, the voice addresses him, "Why are you here, Eliyahu?"

He answers, "I have been zealous for Heaven, for the Israelites have forsaken Your covenant, torn down Your altars, and have put Your prophets to the sword. I alone am left, and they are out to take my life."

Seeing that Eliyahu has not defended the people the way Moshe had, Hashem responds with Eliyahu's final mission, "It is now time to anoint Elisha as your successor."

וְאָמַר רַבִּי חִיָּיא בַּר אַבָּא אָמַר רַבִּי יוֹחָנָן אִלְמָלֵי נִשְׁתַּיֵּיר בִּמְעָרָה שֶׁעָמַד בָּהּ מֹשֶׁה וְאֵלִיָּהוּ כִּמְלֹא נֶקֶב מַחַט סִדְקִית לֹא הָיוּ יְכוֹלִין לַעֲמוֹד מִפְּנֵי הָאוֹרָה שֶׁנֶּאֱמַר כִּי לֹא יִרְאַנִי הָאָדָם וָחָי.

Rabbi Chiya bar Abba cited Rabbi Yochanan: Had there been left open a crack so much as the size of a small sewing needle in the cave in which Moshe and Eliyahu stood, they would not have been able to endure due to the intense light, as it is stated, "For no man shall see Me and live."

Our Sages teach that the cave in which Eliyahu experienced the extraordinary revelation was the same one in which Moshe had felt Hashem's presence.[1] That special cave was fashioned during the Six Days of Creation for the express purpose of Divine revelation for those found worthy. Moshe was the first to merit such an experience. Following his successful appeal to Heaven for forgiveness for the sin of the Golden Calf, Moshe hopes to capitalize on the opportunity of Divine favor and asks Hashem to reveal Himself to Him, as described in *Parashas Ki Sisa*:

And he [Moshe] said, "Please show me Your glory." And He [Hashem] said, "I will make all My goodness pass before you, and I will proclaim the name of Hashem before you; and I will be gracious to whom I will be gracious, and I will show mercy on whom I will show mercy." And He said, "You cannot see My face, for man shall not see Me and live." And Hashem said, "Behold, there is a place by Me, and you shall stand upon the rock. And it shall come to pass, while My glory passes by, that I will put you in a cleft of the rock and will cover you with My hand until I have passed by. And I will take away My hand, and you shall see My back; but My face shall not be seen."

---

1   *Pesachim* 54a.

In both stories, our greatest prophets merit Divine revelation. But they do not see everything because such a revelation would be too powerful for human eyes. Our Sages offer the following analogy: As a king passes through a crowded street, before him walk his bodyguards, who clear the way for him by forcefully moving the people out of the way. A wise individual will make sure he is out of harm's way because the bodyguards will have no mercy on any obstacle in their way.

Similarly, when Hashem in all His glory passes by, as He did for the final plague in Egypt and as He did it when He revealed Himself to Moshe and Eliyahu, it is dangerous to be around. Hashem is accompanied, so to speak, by fiery angels who destroy any obstacle in the way of His path. By placing Moshe and Eliyahu in a tight space in the cleft of the rock or cave, no Divine light was able to enter, and they were protected from any danger posed by the Almighty's entourage.

Imagine how Moshe and Eliyahu must have felt in the tight spaces of their rock clefts. The space was so tight, says Rabbi Yochanan, that there was not so much as a needlepoint's space left for the Divine light to enter. Physically, it was uncomfortable. But of course, they understood that the tightness was there for their protection. They were able to experience the Divine light passing by, but not be harmed by the fiery angels.

Often in life, we find ourselves in tight spots. We feel stressed by the pressures of life. When that happens, look for the crack of Divine light amid all the stress and anxiety. Know that Hashem is surrounding you with His power and revelation. The feeling of intense pressure is there to protect you.

Maybe you're struggling with an approaching examination date. The walls of that pass-or-fail moment are closing in. Your stress levels are rising as that fateful day gets closer and closer. Now you're beginning to think: will you make it to the exam room or will you be so overwhelmed by worry and concern that you won't even reach your destination?

Maybe you're experiencing financial pressures that are making you feel like the walls are closing in. The bills are piling up and you're feeling more and more anxious with each passing hour, day, and week. You've done the math and no matter how you move things around, you just can't meet your obligations. Now, not only are the debts rising, but your stress level is through the roof. The feeling of constriction is unbearable.

If those are the pressures you're feeling, it's not easy to hold on to your faith, but you must. You need to know that Hashem is surrounding you with His light. That pressure is His protection from the intense revelation of blessing He has stored up for you. If He were to reveal it to you, you would not survive, so abundant is His bounty. The pressure is there for you to reach out to Him in prayer and then to inspire you to achieve your very best.

You have unbelievable potential waiting to be released. But our Father in Heaven knows that most of us will not fulfill our potential without a little prodding. That pressure you're feeling is the Almighty's light pushing your back against the wall, forcing you to reveal your innermost strengths and become the person He has created you to be. Just like the man who encounters a lion in the forest and is able to escape at superhuman speed, it's the intense pressure that brings out the very best in us.

If Hashem has placed you in a tight spot, always remind yourself that He is surrounding you with His light. He is protecting you. He is motivating you. And He wants the very best for you. May the pressures of life strengthen your faith in Heaven and help you reach your greatest potential!

Undistracting Your Children

errified, Yosef's brothers stood before him. The second most powerful person in the region had just arrested their youngest brother, Binyamin, accusing him of having stolen the royal goblet. Yehudah begins to intercede on his behalf, even going so far as to offer himself as a slave in exchange for Binyamin's release. Seeing his entreaties failing to make their mark, all of a sudden, Yehudah lets out a mighty roar. The sound is so loud that it is heard all the way back in the Land of Canaan by his nephew Chushim, who picks himself up and sprints down to Egypt. Chushim joins Yehudah and together they let out another great roar. At that point, Yosef decides the time has arrived to reveal his identity to his brothers.[1]

תַּנְיָא רַבִּי יְהוּדָה אוֹמֵר מִשׁוּם רַבִּי אֶלְעָזָר בֶּן עֲזַרְיָה הַקּוֹרֵא אֶת שְׁמַע צָרִיךְ שֶׁיַּשְׁמִיעַ לְאָזְנוֹ שֶׁנֶּאֱמַר שְׁמַע יִשְׂרָאֵל ה' אֱלֹקֵינוּ ה' אֶחָד הַשְׁמַע לְאָזְנֶיךָ מַה שֶּׁאַתָּה מוֹצִיא מִפִּיךָ רַבִּי מֵאִיר אוֹמֵר אֲשֶׁר אָנֹכִי מְצַוְּךָ הַיּוֹם עַל לְבָבֶךָ אַחַר כַּוָּנַת הַלֵּב הֵן הֵן הַדְּבָרִים.

Rabbi Yehudah quoted Rabbi Elazar ben Azaryah: One who recites the Shema must make it audible to his ears, as it is stated, "Hear O Israel, Hashem is our God, Hashem is One." Allow your ears to hear the words you are expressing with your

---

1   *Bereishis Rabbah* 93:7.

mouth. Rabbi Meir says: "Which I command you this day shall
be upon your heart" means "these words," follow the intent of
the heart [even if he doesn't vocalize them to his ears].

The *Kaf Hachaim* asks:[2] What if you're in a noisy room and you can't
hear yourself saying *Shema*? Do you need to raise your voice to a volume audible to your ears right this second or does it suffice to read the
Shema at your regular volume, which would be otherwise sufficiently
audible? According to the *Rambam*, ideally the *Shema* should be audible
to your ears.[3] However, as long as you have vocalized the words, you've
fulfilled your duty.

Nevertheless, the fact that you must vocalize the words is actually
unique to the *Shema*. Most other verbal mitzvos, you still fulfill your
obligation even if you read the words in your head.[4] Why is the *Shema*
different?

The *Shaagas Aryeh* explains that the *Shema's* distinction lies in the
phrase, "*V'shinantam l'vanecha v'dibarta bam*," meaning, "And you shall
teach them to your children and you shall *speak* of them." Since the
Shema explicitly uses the term "speak," verbalizing the words becomes
crucial to the fulfillment of the mitzvah.[5]

Let's return to the *Kaf Hachaim's* question. In the noisy room, how
loud must your *Shema* be? It might not be essential that you hear it
with your own ears. But remember: if the basis of verbalizing the words
is the mitzvah of teaching your children, then you'd better be sure that
your children can hear you above all the other noise in the room. Of
course, I'm not referring to a construction site. I'm talking about all
the "noise" your kids encounter day in and day out in the world around
them. It's not easy to convey the message of Torah when there are so
many distractions drowning out our efforts. But the louder the other
voices are, the stronger our message must be.

---

2   *Orach Chaim* 62:7.
3   *K'rias Shema* 2:8.
4   *Rambam, Berachos* 1:7.
5   *Siman* 6.

Back in the day, you could send your kids to a yeshiva day school or even the local *cheder*, rest assured you'd done your duty as a parent, in terms of conveying our tradition to the next generation. The children attended their classes, they absorbed the material, and we all turned out pretty much the way our parents intended.

Those days are long gone. The "noise level" around our children has skyrocketed. The few hours of Torah they receive each day or each week are no match for the foreign ideas and worldly temptations to which they are exposed on a constant basis. If you want them to hear the message, you're going to have to scream at the top of your lungs to prevail over the volume of non-Torah noise they're hearing.

Now, of course, we're not talking about literal screaming, God forbid. We're talking about finding ways to make the words of Torah just as stimulating and exciting as all the competing interests in their lives. That means spending one-on-one time with them, an investment the likes of which our parents didn't have to make. Every moment you spend learning Torah with them in a fun and engaging manner is one less moment the other voices are able to capture their attention.

While it would be nice to have hours every day to spend with each of your children, for most of us that's just not possible. But if you can find an hour or two, even weekly, to spend with each child, "undistracting" them from all the other noise, you've already gone a long way to raising the volume of what's truly important in life. The quality of those encounters will far outshine the quantity of the distracting influences in their lives.

In fact, it needn't be hour blocks that you spend with them. It could be ten minutes a day. As long as you commit to those ten minutes being nonnegotiable—no matter where in the city or world you find yourself—you will make a major statement to your children and have a lasting impact upon their lives.

It wasn't easy for Yehudah to make himself heard in Egypt. He had to muster up all his strength to capture the attention of the next generation. But when he did, they responded to the call.

There's a lot of noise in the world today. Any parent able to hear himself speak above all the racket is doing well. If your kids can hear you amid all their distractions, then that's even better. May you merit conveying the message of our *mesorah* in a manner that is audible to your children, grandchildren, and generations to come!

Multisensory Mitzvos

The first time Moshe and Aharon visited Pharaoh, it didn't go so well. And so, the next time, they had a few tricks up their sleeves. Surely, miracles would demonstrate to Pharaoh that he would be well advised not to play games with God.

"When Pharaoh speaks to you, saying, 'Show for yourselves a sign,'" instructs the Almighty, "you shall say to Aharon, 'Take your staff and cast it before Pharaoh,' and it shall become a serpent."[1]

Off to Pharaoh's palace they go, confident that this wondrous sign will guarantee a successful mission. They appear before the king and perform the miracle just as Hashem had instructed.

"Seriously?" scoffs Pharaoh. "You call that a trick? Everyone knows how you do that one!" He calls in his magicians who are able to reproduce the staff-to-serpent magic trick.

Indeed, it was a classic Egyptian magic trick. How did they do it? They would take snake skins and have children hide underneath them. They would then throw down their staffs and proceed with misdirecting the audience's attention. Amid this sleight of hand, the children in the snake skins would suddenly appear and grab the "magical" staffs, pretending they were the sticks that had miraculously come to life![2]

---

1   *Shemos* 7:9.
2   *Malbim, Shemos* 7:11.

תָּנוּ רַבָּנָן בַּתּוֹרָה אֶחָד קוֹרֵא וְאֶחָד מְתַרְגֵּם מְתַרְגֵּם וּבִלְבַד שֶׁלֹּא יְהֵא אֶחָד קוֹרֵא
וּשְׁנַיִם מְתַרְגְּמִין וּבַנָּבִיא אֶחָד קוֹרֵא וּשְׁנַיִם מְתַרְגְּמִין וּבִלְבַד שֶׁלֹּא יְהוּ שְׁנַיִם
קוֹרִין וּשְׁנַיִם מְתַרְגְּמִין וּבַהַלֵּל וּבַמְּגִילָה אֲפִילוּ עֲשָׂרָה קוֹרִין וַעֲשָׂרָה מְתַרְגְּמִין
מַאי טַעְמָא כֵּיוָן דַּחֲבִיבָה יָהֲבִי דַּעְתַּיְיהוּ וְשָׁמְעֵי.

The Sages taught: When reading from the Torah, one person
reads and one may translate, provided that there is not one
person reading and two people translating [because two voices
cannot be heard simultaneously]. But when reading from the
Prophets, one person reads and two may translate. This is
the case provided that there are not two people reading and
two translating. And when reciting Hallel and reading the
Megillah, even ten people may read and ten may translate.
What is the reason? Since it is dear [to the people], they will
pay attention and listen.

Why do people love listening to the *Megillah*? *Rashi* explains that it's
the novelty that makes it exciting.[3] Purim only comes around once
a year, and so people look forward to hearing the *Megillah*, which they
haven't picked up in twelve or thirteen months.

But, if that's why we love the *Megillah*, why aren't we as keen about
the Torah reading? After all, it's a different parashah every week. And
we haven't heard this week's story for a whole year! The *Maharach Ohr
Zarua* answers that our lack of enthusiasm arises from the fact that,
while it might be a different parashah, it's still the same Torah that we
read from each week.[4]

A different reason for our *Megillah* excitement is offered by the *Levush*
who ascribes our love for the *Megillah* to the miraculous nature of the
story.[5] But that poses the same problem. The Torah also contains many
miracle stories. Why aren't we equally excited about those miracles?

Let's think about why a miracle is exciting. The truth is, miracles are
not a big deal for Hashem. Whether a jug of oil lasts one day or eight

3   Rosh Hashanah 27a.
4   Siman 42.
5   Levush Hatecheles 488:2, 690:2.

takes no greater Heavenly effort. The definition of a miracle doesn't lie in its degree of ease or difficulty. A miracle is something that goes above and beyond the natural order.

If that's the definition of a miracle, then, in a certain sense, we have the ability to create miracles in our own lives. Every time we go above and beyond the natural order of doing things, we've performed miracles. When you think about it, that's how our Sages designed the *Megillah* reading.

What gets us excited about listening to the *Megillah*? It's true that it's novel. But the novelty is not just the fact that we haven't heard it for an entire year. It's not just about quantity, it's also a matter of quality. When we read the *Megillah*, our Sages have infused the moment with a number of customs and practices that go beyond the natural way of reading our sacred texts. The reading comes to life with a multisensory experience.

All the children wait patiently to drown out Haman's name with their *graggers*. There are four *pesukim* in the reading that everyone recites out loud in unison. The *Megillah* must be folded like a letter and, on the two occasions that we read the word "letter," we shake the *Megillah*. The sons of Haman must be read in one breath. When we encounter the story of the insomniac king, the *baal korei* raises his voice. And, even before we begin reading on Purim morning, the rabbi announces that everyone must remember the other mitzvos of the day—the *mishteh*, *matanos l'evyonim*, and *mishloach manos*. Because the *Megillah* appeals to so many of our senses, we love it and pay more attention than we would to a regular Torah reading.

The same is true of the most widespread mitzvah, the Pesach Seder. There is hardly a Jew in the world who does not sit down and have some semblance of a Seder, even if it's just a bite of matzah and a cup of wine to mark the occasion. And sometimes we're talking about people who have not so much as set foot in a shul in many years. Why do they do Pesach?

Just like the *Megillah*, Pesach's distinction lies in its ability to deliver an exciting experience in a variety of ways. The Seder was designed to cater to every learning style. Are you a visual learner? Well, look at the

Seder plate we've prepared for you! Are you a musical learner? Well, even those who don't know the words "*Shema Yisrael*," probably know "*Dayeinu*." Gustatory learner? Well, we have everything from good wine to bitter herbs that will set your mouth on fire.

Whatever your learning style, there's something for everyone on Pesach. And that's why nearly every Jewish person feels some kind of affinity to the holiday. Our Sages created a multisensory experiential learning event that speaks to every individual, which is particularly important when we are dealing with the annual occasion designated to "tell your child" about our national history and heritage.

When you love learning, it doesn't feel like learning. It becomes entertaining! And everybody loves entertainment. Pesach and Purim are the ultimate models of Jewish learning. Our Sages have already done most of the heavy lifting for us on those two festivals. The challenge for each and every one of us is taking the multisensory model of engagement they've demonstrated and applying it to other mitzvos as we endeavor to teach our children and pass on our heritage to the next generation. That's not to say we shouldn't create new and exciting innovative ideas for our family Seders. If you feel that adds to the experience, that's wonderful!

But now, take that same creativity you've shown on Pesach and bring it to your weekly Shabbos table. When our daughter Miriam Leah became bas mitzvah, she designed table centerpieces for each parashah of the year and placed them on each table at the *simchah*. We later met a family who makes special parashah-inspired table designs every week of the year. Most of us rush to set the Shabbos table just before candle lighting. That special family would start on Sunday with a family meeting where they would plan the design for the Shabbos table six days later!

Every mitzvah we do has multiple entry points. The challenge is to create the feeling of excitement and novelty throughout our spiritual lives. Today, even Torah learning has multisensory opportunities for engagement. Are you an avid self-learning reader? Well, there's no shortage of text today in our age of print, both classic *sefarim* and online Torah essays. Are you more visual or auditory? Attend a Torah class or watch or listen to one online! Are you a social learner? Find a *chavrusa* to learn with! Whatever your learning style, there's something out there for you.

The *Levush* says we love the *Megillah* because it's miraculous. In truth, you could read the *Megillah* and see nothing miraculous in the story at all. It's miraculous when we make it miraculous. When we recognize the supernatural order of events by reading it in a way that transcends our mundane reading of a text, we demonstrate our belief in the miracle.

When Moshe appeared before Pharaoh, he performed a miracle. Pharaoh responded with his own demonstration of the supernatural. He knew that it was nothing more than sleight of hand. But it certainly brought out the oohs and aahs from the crowd. If Pharaoh could perform "miracles" using his black magic, you certainly have the Divine gift to make every moment miraculous!

You have the power to make Torah and mitzvos not just exciting, but supernatural. Do something extraordinary and you will imbue passion in your children and even your own *avodas Hashem*. May you be inspired with the wow factor to make Torah and mitzvos forever dear to you and your children!

Annoying Latecomers

R abbi Yaakov Yosef of Polnoye was once invited to be the *sandek* at a bris in a small village near his town. He arrives at the designated hour but there's no minyan. They're waiting and waiting, but it's taking forever for the people to arrive. Six men. Then seven. A while later, eight. With each passing minute, the rabbi is beginning to lose his patience. He tells them politely that he has other commitments and he'll really need to leave shortly. The ninth man arrives. But the time is dragging on and the rabbi's patience is wearing thin. He apologizes and tells them they'll have to find another *sandek*. He's getting up to leave, when all of a sudden, in the distance they spot an old man walking along the road adjacent to the village. They send one of the youth to catch him and try to secure him as a tenth man. He tells them that he really was en route to town, but if he's needed, "so be it."

After the bris, they offer the stranger something to eat. "I really need to get going," he replies, "but so be it." And each time they offer him something else, his response is, "So be it."

As he's about to depart, they ask him to explain his peculiar expression. He tells them, "I live by the verse, '*Ashrei ha'am she'kachah lo*—Happy are the people who have it so.' I understand the verse as such: Happy are the people who are able to say about anything that happens in their life, '*kachah*—so—be it,' meaning, they have the patience to accept anything

Hashem sends their way calmly, knowing that this is the very best for them." And then as quickly as he had appeared, the old man is gone.

Upon hearing these wise words, Rabbi Yaakov Yosef turns to those assembled and exclaims, "That man must have been Eliyahu HaNavi, who comes to every bris. Heaven decided I needed to hear that message so I would learn to stop rushing from one task to the next important event. Clearly, Hashem wanted me to be right here, knowing that there's nowhere more important for me to be right now."[1]

תַּנְיָא הַקּוֹרֵא בַּתּוֹרָה לֹא יִפְחוֹת מִשְּׁלֹשָׁה פְּסוּקִים וְאִיתְּמַר עֲלָה רַב אָמַר דּוֹלֵג וּשְׁמוּאֵל אָמַר פּוֹסֵק רַב אָמַר דּוֹלֵג מַאי טַעְמָא לָא אָמַר פּוֹסֵק קָסָבַר כָּל פְּסוּקָא דְּלָא פַּסְקֵיהּ מֹשֶׁה אֲנַן לָא פָּסְקִינַן לֵיהּ וּשְׁמוּאֵל אָמַר פּוֹסֵק מַאי טַעְמָא לָא אָמַר דּוֹלֵג גְּזֵירָה מִשּׁוּם הַנִּכְנָסִין וּמִשּׁוּם הַיּוֹצְאִין.

רַשִׁ"י: גְּזֵירָה מִשּׁוּם הַנִּכְנָסִין—שֶׁיִּשְׁמְעוּ הַשֵּׁנִי מַתְחִיל פָּסוּק זֶה וְיֹאמְרוּ לֹא קָרָא רִאשׁוֹן אֶלָּא שְׁנַיִם וְכֵן הַיּוֹצְאִין שֶׁיִּשְׁמְעוּ אֶת הָרִאשׁוֹן קוֹרֵא שְׁלֹשָׁה וְיֵצְאוּ מִבֵּית הַכְּנֶסֶת וְיֹאמְרוּ לֹא יִקְרָא הַשֵּׁנִי אֶלָּא שְׁנַיִם.

One who reads from the Torah should not read fewer than three verses. And it was stated [with regard to an eight-verse paragraph], Rav said: The next reader repeats the previous verse. And Shmuel said: The first reader divides the third verse and reads half of it, and the second reader begins with the second half. Rav said he repeats. What is the reason that he did not state that the first reader divides? He maintains that any verse that Moshe did not divide, we may not divide. And Shmuel said: The first reader divides. What is the reason that he did not state that the second reader repeats? A decree was enacted on account of those who enter late or leave early.

Rashi: Latecomers might hear the second reader begin at the third verse and assume the first reader only read two verses. Similarly, the early leavers might hear the first reader read three verses and then leave assuming that the next reader will only read the remaining two verses.

---

1   Horowitz, *Otzar Sippurim L'Mechanchim* 2:381.

How do you divide eight into three equal whole-number parts? As the Gemara says, we encounter this challenge every Rosh Chodesh. We have four people to call up. In the first paragraph, however, there are only eight verses, which need to be divided between three *aliyos*. And so we utilize Rav's solution and repeat the third verse.

Why doesn't Shmuel recommend the repetition of a verse? Just in case someone is tardy and might mistakenly believe that the first *aliyah* was short. Listen to the incredible sensitivity of our Sages. According to Shmuel, they were willing to design the halachah and the whole structure of the Torah reading to accommodate the misunderstanding of some ignorant fellow who sleeps in and wanders into shul late!

You know the feeling when you walk into a lecture or class late and you have a question? Most of us wouldn't raise our hands. After all, maybe the lecturer already dealt with that issue before you got there, right? Not Shloimy. When I was in yeshiva, Shloimy would almost always come late to *shiur*. Inevitably, five minutes after arriving, his hand would shoot up and he would ask a question that the Rosh Yeshiva had already dealt with before he got there. But the Rosh Yeshiva would patiently respond to him as if he had just asked the most novel and clever question imaginable.

One day, my *chavrusa* Nussy had enough and blurted out what we were all thinking, "If you'd simply get here on time, you'd have the answers to all your questions!"

What's our typical response to people who, like Shloimy, lack this basic social awareness? Most people would react like Nussy did, with impatience and dismissiveness. But that's not the way of our Sages. They bent over backward to accommodate these "schleppers," making sure they would not be left with any misunderstandings. And it was in this great tradition of our Sages that the Rosh Yeshiva would calmly answer Shloimy's questions without making him feel in any way inadequate or embarrassed for his poor social awareness.

The Shloimys of the world don't just show up late to shul or yeshiva. They can appear anytime and anywhere. They're the people who will enter a conversation at a social gathering and make the least helpful contribution to the conversation. They've just arrived, but you've been speaking about that matter for the last ten minutes! Your initial reaction might be to disregard them, but our Sages teach us to smile warmly and ensure that they do not feel the least bit slighted. And when others roll their eyes, your challenge is then to work even harder to include them into the conversation.

The world contains many different kinds of people. Some show up late, some leave early, some ask ridiculous questions, some lack basic social awareness. It's tempting to be dismissive of their shortcomings. But if Hashem has brought them into your life, He is presenting you with a challenge. He wants to see how you will deal with this "annoying" person. It's easy to say, "They should get their act together and come on time." But that's not your issue. Your task is to make them feel cherished and respected even when you are unimpressed with them.

And sometimes, like when Rabbi Yaakov Yosef was waiting at the bris, it's not just that they're annoying with their tardiness, they might be causing you significant inconvenience. When that happens, it's not easy to maintain your patience. But that's the test that Hashem is sending your way. It goes without saying that the attitude and behavior of these latecomers leave much to be desired. They most certainly need to work on themselves. But one cannot help but be moved by the extraordinary way our Sages worked the halachah around accommodating even those people who didn't seem to being pulling their weight in the community. And that should be a lesson to us all.

Imagine the Prince of Wales walked into shul in the middle of *leining*. Would you turn up your nose at him and wonder why he couldn't get out of bed on time? Of course not. You would treat him with the utmost honor. It should be obvious to us then that when a child of the Supreme King of Kings walks into shul a little late, you must likewise treat him with the utmost respect and dignity. May you forever strive to attain the sensitivity of our Sages toward every individual, regardless of how far they have yet to travel along their spiritual and sociopsychological journey!

Unfinished Business

The Israelites are wandering through the wilderness and Hashem declares, "And they shall build for Me a sanctuary and I shall dwell among them." Detailed instructions are then conveyed and the people begin to fret.

"We're in the middle of the desert!" they cry. "Where does God expect us to find all the materials to build a Tabernacle?"

"Look at all the gold and silver He blessed you with as you left Egypt," Moshe responds. "Surely, you can part with some of those riches!"

"Yes, but what about building materials?" they ask. "There are no trees here in the desert. Where will the wood come from?"

"Fear not," says Moshe, "I have brought cedar wood from Egypt."

"Cedar wood?" ask the Israelites incredulously. "There were no cedar trees in Egypt!"

"Yes, there were," Moshe replies. "They were planted by our forefather Yaakov, in preparation for this very day!"

"But where did he get cedar trees to plant?" the people inquire.

"That's a good question," says Moshe. "Avraham Avinu planted them originally in Be'er Sheva. Yaakov later stopped by to pick up some of Avraham's trees. He brought them to Egypt and replanted them. And now we have the wood for the Tabernacle."

מַתְנִי׳ אֵין פּוֹרְסִין עַל שְׁמַע וְאֵין עוֹבְרִין לִפְנֵי הַתֵּיבָה וְאֵין נוֹשְׂאִין אֶת כַּפֵּיהֶם וְאֵין קוֹרִין בַּתּוֹרָה וְאֵין מַפְטִירִין בַּנָּבִיא פָּחוֹת מֵעֲשָׂרָה.

תוספות: אין פורסין על שמע פחות מעשרה—בירושלמי מפרש שאם
התחילו בעשרה ויצאו מקצתן אפ״ה גומרין ועל היוצאים הוא אומר ועוזבי
ה׳ יכלו (ישעיהו א׳, כ״ח) וכן הלכה.

*We may not recite Kaddish and Barchu before Shema, nor may
we do Chazaras Ha'shatz, nor may we duchen, nor may we lein
or recite the haftarah…with less than a minyan.*

*Tosafos: The Yerushalmi explains that if they began with ten
and some left, nonetheless they may complete the service.
And concerning those who leave, it says, "And those who leave
Hashem shall be finished off." And such is the halachah.*

Let's say the chazzan starts his repetition with a minyan present
and then one fellow needs to run out to work. The halachah is that
the chazzan finishes *Chazaras Ha'shatz* and the congregation may even
recite *Kedushah*, even though they're short of a minyan.[1] On the one
hand, that's quite helpful in shuls where the minyan is tight. On the
other hand, it seems to be a double-edged sword. According to *Tosafos*,
if you leave early, you'll be finished off! Given the dire consequences
of slipping out early, why would anyone want to come to shul in the
first place?

Sometimes in life, we're afraid to embark on a task for fear that we
will be unable to complete the job. The *Yerushalmi*'s message is that we
should never be put off by such fears. We must start the work, and the
Almighty will ensure that the job gets done. In the case of the fellow
who leaves shul for work, the *Chazon Ish* maintains that despite the
appearance of only nine men, the minyan remains completely intact.[2]
The presence of the Shechinah manifest in a minyan stays in the room,
even if the human beings are unable to be physically present!

If that's the case, what is the connection to Yeshayahu's prophecy,
"And those who leave Hashem shall be finished off"? Most of us are
familiar with the word "finish" as we read it every Friday night. "And the
Heavens and Earth and all their hosts were finished. And God finished

1   *Shulchan Aruch, Orach Chaim* 55:3.
2   Ibid., *Orach Chaim* 137:5.

on the seventh the work He had done." The connotation is more one of "completion." Hashem completed the creation of the universe.

In fact, the *mefarshim* offer a variety of translations and meanings of the word "finished," which point to its mysterious power that goes above and beyond the mere idea of completion. The *Targum Yerushalmi* understands the word to connote "desire,"[3] while *Targum Onkelos* suggests that the idea being expressed is that "the Creation was in a state of unparalleled beauty and splendor."[4]

If that's the meaning of the word, the quotation from Yeshayahu aims to teach us a powerful lesson about leaving early. On the odd occasion, you might find yourself unavoidably having to leave Hashem's presence, but you will complete the task nonetheless. Had you never appeared to begin with, the *tefillah b'tzibbur* would not have begun to happen. Now that you've made the effort to show up, you've brought the Shechinah into the shul. And, even in your absence, you will complete the task. Your efforts are certainly "desirable" to Hashem and reflect "unparalleled beauty and splendor" in His eyes.

The same is true of other communal responsibilities people avoid because they cannot complete the task. For example, I might ask a shul member to join the Purim committee.

"Sorry, Rabbi, I'm leaving on vacation to Florida just before Purim."

"Well, maybe you could help out with the design and planning? You always bring such great ideas to the table!"

"But, Rabbi, I don't feel right committing if I can't be there to see the project through to its completion."

The message of *Tosafos* is that if you are part of the initial quorum, Hashem considers it as if you were there to complete the task. You may be basking in the Florida sun, but as far as Hashem is concerned, you're at the Purim event in shul!

In *Pirkei Avos*, Rabbi Tarfon teaches, "It is not incumbent upon you to finish the job, nor are you free to desist from it."[5] According to the

---

3   Cited in *Baal Haturim, Bereishis* 2:2.
4   *Haamek Davar, Bereishis* 2:1.
5   *Avos* 2:16.

Ahavah B'Taanugim, the Mishnah means that while we are tasked with starting a mitzvah, Hashem will always ensure it is completed.

Avraham knew he wouldn't be the one to finish the building of the Tabernacle. Likewise, his grandson Yaakov knew that he wouldn't complete the task. Nonetheless, they did not desist from starting the job. Often in life, the most difficult part of a project is getting it off the ground. Without the efforts of our patriarchs, can you imagine how impossible the construction of the Tabernacle would have felt to the Children of Israel? But once they had all the pieces in place, it was simply a matter of completing the task their forefathers had begun many years earlier.

Never avoid engaging in mitzvos because you are worried you will not be able to complete them. You can and will complete the task. Physically you might not be able to be there to the end, but our Father in Heaven will reward you with the merit of its completion. May you constantly embark on mitzvah projects and trust that, if you can't complete them, Hashem will complete them for you!

DAF 24

Incentivizing Mitzvos

Rabbi Akiva once encountered a man carrying a load heavy enough for ten men to carry. To say that the man looked weary as he ran to and fro would have been a massive understatement. The poor fellow looked like he was about to collapse from exhaustion.

"Why do you do such arduous work?" Rabbi Akiva asked the man.

"I am not of this world," the man replied. "This is my punishment for my sins when I was alive. Every day I must chop and gather wood. The wood is then lit and I am consumed by its fire."

"What did you do to deserve such an awful sentence?" inquired Rabbi Akiva.

"I was a tax collector in Ludkia," said the man, "but I was lax with the rich and oppressive with the poor."

"Is there any way at all, my son," asked Rabbi Akiva, "that your sentence might be commuted?"

"I have heard that if my son were to recite Kaddish or read the haftarah, my soul would be saved. But alas, I died before I was able to meet my child. My wife, at the time of my passing, was pregnant. Now, indeed I have a son, but there is nobody to instruct him."

Rabbi Akiva set off immediately to Ludkia and found the boy whose father had died shortly prior to his birth. He taught him Kaddish and he recited the prayer in shul. That night, the tortured soul appeared to

Rabbi Akiva in a dream. He informed him that he had been freed from his sentence and he blessed Rabbi Akiva.[1]

מַתְנִי' הַמַּפְטִיר בַּנָּבִיא הוּא פּוֹרֵס עַל שְׁמַע וְהוּא עוֹבֵר לִפְנֵי הַתֵּיבָה וְהוּא נוֹשֵׂא אֶת כַּפָּיו: גְּמ' מַאי טַעְמָא רַב פָּפָּא אָמַר מִשּׁוּם כָּבוֹד רַבָּה בַּר שִׁימִי אָמַר מִשּׁוּם דְּאָתֵי לְאִינְצוּיֵי.

Mishnah: The person called up for maftir also gets to be the chazzan for Shema and Shemoneh Esreh, and if he is a Kohen he leads the duchening.

Gemara: What is the reason? Rav Pappa said: To grant him honor. Rabbah bar Shimi said: Lest they start a fight.

Our Mishnah is worried about the fellow who receives the *maftir aliyah*. In order that he shouldn't feel slighted we make sure to give him something else like leading *Shacharis*. But why would someone feel bad about getting *maftir*? Ask any *gabbai* and they'll tell you it's the most coveted *aliyah*! Clearly then, in Talmudic times, the *maftir* was not particularly desirable.

What was the reason for its lack of appeal? It boils down to the fact that *maftir* was actually an invented extra *aliyah*. At an earlier point in our history, the Roman authorities prohibited the Torah reading. In response, our Sages instituted that we should read a corresponding portion from the *Neviim*.[2] Once the decree was annulled, the Rabbis decided that the *Navi* reading should remain. After all, outside of the haftarah reading, most people learn very little Tanach!

In order to formalize the reading and connect it to the Torah portion, they instituted that the *maftir*—the person reading the haftarah—should also be called to the Torah. In order to demonstrate that it was connected, but distinct, it became an eighth *aliyah*. It was tacked on to the first seven and fashioned in a manner whereby the reader would repeat the final few verses of the *sedrah*, a piece that was already *leined* by the previous honoree. So you can understand why

---

1   See *Yoreh Deah* 376, *Beis Yosef* and *Darkei Moshe*.
2   *Mishnah Berurah* 284:2.

people might have felt slighted to receive the addendum or afterthought *aliyah*, or why getting *maftir* might even have led to fights in shul. The Rabbis' solution was ingenious: whoever gets *maftir* will also get to lead *Shacharis*. Problem solved.

Now, watch what happened somewhere over the centuries. As the story of Rabbi Akiva's encounter with the dead man circulated, the desirability of the *maftir aliyah* skyrocketed. First it started with *aveilim*, those in mourning for their deceased parents. It then expanded to observers of yahrzeits, and then it eventually became the *aliyah* of choice for bar mitzvah boys and *chassanim*![3]

Nowadays, everyone wants the *maftir*. In fact, if you look into the later *poskim*, you'll find rationales for why *maftir* is the finest *aliyah*, such as the fact that it involves the public chanting of additional *berachos*.[4] So now, instead of needing to compensate the *maftir* with other incentives, we've raised the inherent value of the *maftir* and made it a prized commodity.

The truth is, the *maftir* should never have needed rehabilitation. After all, when you think about it, whoever received the *maftir aliyah* was given greater honor than any of the members of the *tzibbur* who weren't even called up to begin with! The recipient should have been grateful for his *kibbud*, regardless of how it ranked compared to the other *aliyos*. But sadly, that's not how the human psyche works. We're quite content sitting in shul as a participant. But the second we get an *aliyah*, we suddenly start comparing our *kibbud* to everybody else's, instead of simply thanking the *gabbai* for the opportunity to bless the Torah in any way, shape, or form.

And so, to begin with, the *maftir* was incentivized. Until, ultimately, our Sages were able to demonstrate that receiving *maftir* was not to be spurned. And they were so successful that people nowadays chase after the opportunity to read the haftarah!

That's really the process of maturity that accompanies us through life's journey along the path of Torah and mitzvos. In order to motivate

---

3   See *Shu"t Tzitz Eliezer* 21:20.
4   *Pri Megadim Eshel Avraham* 147:11; *Vayaan Avraham* (A. Palagi), *Yoreh Deah* 36.

children to learn Torah, we need to incentivize them. They're not running to class because they don't appreciate the importance of Torah. And so we offer them prizes and allowance money to get them to attend after-school cheder. I'll never forget the ice pops we used to receive as kids at Sydney Yeshiva Cheder or the "cheder biscuits" they would hand out to us at Adass Cheder.

As we get older, the hope is that we are able to develop a maturity whereby we understand the inherent value of Torah and mitzvos. Nobody should need to incentivize a mature adult to come to shul or attend a *shiur*. We come because we know that we're receiving the ultimate reward—the ability to connect with the Master of the Universe!

Imagine a parent who gave candy to his adult child every time that child passed an exam at medical school. Of course, that would be ridiculous. When she was a little child, it made sense to reward her with sweets for paying attention and doing well at school. But, hopefully, by the time she's reached medical school, she understands the importance of what she's doing and no longer requires external validation and motivation.

Unfortunately, some of us are slow to mature spiritually. We might not need cheder biscuits to incentivize our *shiur* attendance. But we still feel burdened by our dedication to Torah and mitzvos. And so we console ourselves with the comforting knowledge that God will reward us in *Olam Haba*. But that shouldn't be our motive. Torah and mitzvos are inherently valuable. There is no greater, more fulfilling, more meaningful task we could be engaged with in this world than connecting with Heaven. When we learn Torah and do mitzvos, we unite ourselves with the Almighty!

The time and effort spent on Torah and mitzvos should be the most exciting, exhilarating area of our lives. Everything else is merely a vehicle to reach the ultimate goal of spiritual engagement. If you're not feeling the passion of Torah and mitzvos, maybe you need to refocus. Returning to our medical school example, think about the student who still needs the candy or pocket money from her parents to incentivize her to pass her exams. Clearly, her heart isn't in it. So what should she do? Find an alternative career to train in that will get her moving and inspired.

Similarly, with Torah study, if you're not excited about the *shiur* you're attending, find another one. We all have different *shorshei neshamah*, soul roots. Some of us will love learning *mussar*, others will prefer Tanach. Don't bow to the peer pressure of which area of Torah is the best or most popular. "Medical school" is not for everyone. Likewise, with mitzvos, if shul committees aren't your thing, perhaps *bikur cholim* is more up your *neshamah*'s alley. If public challah bakes don't do it for you, maybe helping out at a youth shelter is more your thing.

Torah and mitzvos are the most valuable commodities on Earth. They don't need incentives; they are diamonds waiting to be gathered. May you quickly discover your area of spiritual passion!

DAF 25

A Wicked Blessing

Yaakov has spent many years at his uncle Lavan's house in Charan. Now it's time to return home to the Land of Israel. He knows that the next great showdown will be his reunion with his brother Eisav. But before he meets Eisav, a mysterious incident occurs. Yaakov meets an angel and spends the night wrestling with him. All night long they wrestle until the break of dawn. The angel realizes that he cannot overpower Yaakov, but he is able to dislocate his hip bone.

The angel then cries out, "Let me go because dawn has broken!"

Yaakov responds, "I will not let you go unless you bless me."

"What is your name?" asks the angel.

"Yaakov," the patriarch responds.

"No longer will your name be Yaakov," declares the angel. "Rather, you shall be called Yisrael, for you have overpowered God and man, and you have prevailed."

Why did Yaakov request a blessing from an angel that had harmed him?

הָאוֹמֵר יְבָרְכוּךְ טוֹבִים הֲרֵי זוֹ דֶּרֶךְ הַמִּינוּת.

רש״י: יברכוך טובים ה״ז דרך מינות—שאינו כולל רשעים בשבחו של מקום וחכמים למדו (כריתות דף ו:) מחלבנה שריחה רע ומנאה הכתוב בין סממני הקטורת שמצריכן הכתוב בהרצאתן להיותן באגודה אחת.

94

The Mishnah states: One who says, "May the good people bless You," is speaking heretically.

Rashi: He is not including wicked people in his praise of the Almighty. Our Sages learned from the inclusion of galbanum—a foul-smelling spice—among the ingredients of the holy incense, that the Torah required all to be included together.

Rav Chaim Kanievsky asks how Yaakov was permitted to ask the angel for a *berachah*. He cites the Vilna Gaon, who disapproved of the third stanza in our Friday night *Shalom Aleichem*, where we ask the angels to bless us. In Judaism, we need not appeal to intermediaries such as angels for spiritual sustenance; we have a direct line to Hashem! He answers that having injured Yaakov, the angel now owed him something. Yaakov was entitled to payment for damages. And so he demanded his due in the form of a blessing.[1]

You'd have thought that Yaakov would have wanted to run away from that dangerous angel as quickly as possible. He'd already caused him harm and now he was ready to disappear. And yet Yaakov saw the moment as an opportunity of Divine blessing. Not in spite of the damage he'd caused him, rather because of it!

In life, when people cause you harm, you have four possible responses. You could try to damage them back. You could run away from them as quickly as possible. You could stick around and bite your lip. Or you could see them as a source of blessing. Let's examine each of these responses.

Human nature would be to take the first route. If someone has been injurious to you, then it's only logical to want to act with contempt toward him. But as the *Sefer Hachinuch* explains, "Everything that happens to him—good and bad—the cause of it coming to him is from God, blessed be He. And from the hand of man—from the hand of a man to his brother—there would not be anything without the will of God." Therefore, concludes the *Chinuch*, there's never any reason to

---

1   *Taama D'Kra*, p. 42.

take revenge against any other person. If someone has injured you, that was the will of God, and you should turn your eyes Heavenward to deal with the matter. For that person's part, he will also have to answer to Heaven for his actions, but that is not your concern.[2]

The second response is to run away. That was Yaakov's initial response to the wrath of his brother Eisav. Instead of dealing with the matter, he ran away to Charan. Now, many years later, he understood that running from one's issues doesn't solve anything. He had escaped the clutches of one menace only to find himself in the hands of another. And so, even when the angel wants to escape, he says, "Not so fast."

The third response is to stay and bite your lip. Most of us believe that doing so is the most righteous response. Despite whatever harm the other person has caused you, you don't respond. You know better than to stoop to his level. If that person is unable to do the right thing, that's his problem. You'll be the better person and take the high moral ground.

But that's not the ultimate response. How did Yaakov respond when he was harmed? He asked the injurer for a blessing. Why would he have done that? Because he understood that harm does not come for no reason. This harm would be the source of his blessing. That's the fourth and ideal response when someone harms you. Recognize the blessing that is about to come forth from that person's act and thank him for it.

What does that mean?

Think back to when someone in your life did something bad that appeared, at the time, to ruin everything. Now think about the way Heaven moved your life along as a result of that occurrence. If things worked out for the best, you really owe a debt of gratitude to the individual who pushed your life in an unexpected direction.

Maybe you had a colleague you couldn't work with. At the time, life felt unbearable. Perhaps it was so unbearable that you ended up leaving that job. And you were upset at that colleague. Every day he made your life miserable, but then you found a better job, a position with far greater potential for career growth. When you think about it, if it were

---

2   *Mitzvah* 241.

not for your unhappiness at the first place, you'd never have looked for that incredible opportunity. And so, rather than be upset at your former colleague, you really owe him the world!

Now, think about whatever challenges you're facing right now and try to transport yourself ahead in time. Try to imagine that the person causing you anxiety in your life today might really be the catalyst for amazing things to come. Maybe that person is forcing you to make certain decisions that you wouldn't have made otherwise. And then the Almighty will propel you to heights you never dreamed of reaching.

Okay, now come back to the present. Take another look at that person who's giving you a hard time. If he's the cause of those great places to which the Almighty is about to take you, then shouldn't you be acting graciously toward him? Rather than showing him disdain, you should be displaying an extraordinarily joyful countenance toward him!

That's the meaning of our Mishnah. If you believe that blessing only comes from righteous people, then you're thinking heretically. Hashem can make anybody the vehicle of His blessings in this world. If you think you're experiencing curses from a person you consider not entirely righteous, you're guilty of attributing the circumstances that are happening to you as occurring beyond Hashem's dominion. That's heretical. The right way to approach the challenges of the wicked is to double down on your belief in Hashem's hidden Hand of blessing in your life.

When we picture Yosef being cast into the pit by his brothers, we imagine him cursing them, as they drag him across the field kicking and screaming. We probably think of him sitting in the pit hurling up hateful epithets in their direction, equally angry at them and God. But, ultimately, the pit was his first step on the journey to becoming viceroy of Egypt and being responsible for the sustenance and salvation of the entire region. When his brothers would later plead for grace and mercy, he responded that their actions had only hastened his ascent to royalty. He had no reason to feel vengeful toward them. On the contrary, he was indebted to them for the blessings that they had brought to his life.

Now, let's rewind the clock years earlier and return to the scene of Yosef sitting in the pit. Viewed through the lens of our imperfect *emunah*, we imagined him wallowing in his misery deep down inside the pit.

But Yosef was a *tzaddik*. A *tzaddik* doesn't fret. A *tzaddik* doesn't dwell on his hatred. When everything seems hopeless, the *tzaddik* thanks his oppressors for sending him on a journey to greatness, comforted by the faith that the Almighty does not forsake His loved ones.

The fourth response isn't easy. It entails almost superhuman *bitachon*. But when you live your life with complete faith that Hashem is in control, you begin to see blessings emanate from even the most unlikely sources. May you always believe that all people have the power to be a vehicle for Hashem's blessing!

Opening the Shul to Nonmembers

Moshe was a faithful leader of the Children of Israel. He had miraculously led them out of slavery in Egypt. He had crossed them over the Red Sea on dry land. He had brought the Torah to them. He had led them through the wilderness, ensuring their every need was taken care of. Sadly, however, that was insufficient proof of his Divine mission for his wicked cousin Korach.

Gathering 250 followers, Korach led a rebellion against Moshe, focusing on leadership issues generally and the high priesthood specifically.

"You've appointed your own brother as the Kohen Gadol," Korach challenged Moshe. "Clearly, you've decided to keep the highest honors within your immediate family. Are we not all holy?"

Moshe responded with a test to prove who God had ordained to be the Kohen Gadol. "Tomorrow, you will all appear with pans containing incense. Whoever's incense Hashem will accept, he is the one who has been chosen!"

The next day, they all arrived with their pans. Defiantly, they did not wait until entering the Tabernacle. They placed their incense inside the pans and stood there sneering at Moshe.

Moshe turned his eyes Heavenward and asked Hashem to perform a miracle, an historic moment that would demonstrate undeniably that Moshe and Aharon had indeed been chosen by God. Suddenly, the earth opened up and swallowed Korach and his closest adherents, as the terrified nation looked on. But that wasn't all. A Heavenly fire then swallowed the 250 followers of Korach who had offered the foreign incense.

Aharon's son Elazar then gathered the 250 pans and hammered them out. He fashioned the sheet of metal into a covering for the holy Altar. For the pans had been designated for a holy assignment and now could not be utilized for a mundane purpose.

בְּנֵי הָעִיר שֶׁמָּכְרוּ רְחוֹבָה שֶׁל עִיר לוֹקְחִין בְּדָמָיו בֵּית הַכְּנֶסֶת בֵּית הַכְּנֶסֶת לוֹקְחִין תֵּיבָה תֵּיבָה לוֹקְחִין מִטְפָּחוֹת מִטְפָּחוֹת יִקְחוּ סְפָרִים סְפָרִים לוֹקְחִין תּוֹרָה אֲבָל אִם מָכְרוּ תּוֹרָה לֹא יִקְחוּ סְפָרִים סְפָרִים לֹא יִקְחוּ מִטְפָּחוֹת מִטְפָּחוֹת לֹא יִקְחוּ תֵּיבָה תֵּיבָה לֹא יִקְחוּ בֵּית הַכְּנֶסֶת בֵּית הַכְּנֶסֶת לֹא יִקְחוּ אֶת הָרְחוֹב וְכֵן בְּמוֹתְרֵיהֶן: גְּמ' אָמַר רַבִּי שְׁמוּאֵל בַּר נַחְמָנִי אָמַר רַבִּי יוֹנָתָן לֹא שָׁנוּ אֶלָּא בֵּית הַכְּנֶסֶת שֶׁל כְּפָרִים אֲבָל בֵּית הַכְּנֶסֶת שֶׁל כְּרַכִּין כֵּיוָן דְּמֵעָלְמָא אָתוּ לֵיהּ לָא מָצוּ מְזַבְּנִי לֵיהּ דְּהָוָה לֵיהּ דְּרַבִּים.

רש״י: אבל מכרו תורה כו׳—שמעלין בקדש ולא מורידין. תוספתא מעלין בקדש דכתיב ויקם משה את המשכן (שמות מ׳, י״ח) בצלאל עשה ומשה שהיה גדול ממנו הקימו ולא מורידים דכתיב את מחתות החטאים האלה בנפשותם ועשו אותם רקועי פחים צפוי למזבח כי הקריבום לפני ה׳ ויקדשו וגו' (במדבר י״ז, ג׳) כיון שהוקדשו הוקדשו עד כאן.

Mishnah: If the townsfolk sold the town square, they may use the funds to purchase a synagogue. If they sold the synagogue, they may use the funds to purchase an ark. If they sold the ark, they may use the funds to purchase Torah covers. If they sold the Torah covers, they may purchase holy books of Scripture. If they sold the holy books, they may purchase a Torah scroll. If, however, they sold a Torah, they may not use the funds to purchase holy books; holy books, they may not purchase Torah covers; Torah covers, they may not purchase an ark; ark, they may not purchase a synagogue; and synagogue, they may not purchase a square. And same is true of the leftover funds.

Rashi: We ascend in holiness and do not descend. [Therefore, the proceeds of the sale of a holy item must be used to purchase a holier item.] The Tosefta derives the principle of ascending in holiness from, "And Moshe erected the Tabernacle." Betzalel made it, and Moshe, who was greater than him, erected it. And the principle of not descending is derived from, "The fire pans of those who sinned at the cost of their lives, let them be made into hammered sheets as plating for the Altar, for they have been used for offering to Hashem and been sanctified." Once they have been sanctified, they are sanctified.

Gemara: Rabbi Shmuel bar Nachmeni quotes Rabbi Yonasan: When is it permissible to sell a synagogue and use the funds to purchase an ark? It is only when we are dealing with a synagogue in a village. Concerning a city synagogue, however, since people come from far and wide to pray there, it may not be sold because it belongs to the public.

There's a classic story told of the fellow who shows up to shul one Rosh Hashanah. He is greeted at the entrance and asked for his ticket.

"I don't have a ticket," the man responds.

"Well, I'm sorry then, I can't admit you. We only allow members to pray here," he is told.

"Please, sir," the visitor pleads. "My brother is a member and I have an important message to convey to him from our mother."

The greeter looks the visitor up and down and acquiesces reluctantly. "Fine," he says. "You have five minutes to go and pass the message on to your brother. But I'm warning you: Don't let me catch you davening!"

While this anecdote might sound a little over the top, many shuls struggle with their policy toward nonmembers. Should they allow nonmembers to utilize their services? Some people have no problem showing up every Shabbos, or even every day, without ever paying a penny toward the upkeep of the shul. How do they think the lights stay on? Where do they think the mortgage payments come from? These are questions that don't seem to bother them.

But it does bother many of the members of the shul. Ask anyone who has served on a shul board, and they will attest to the fact that this is one of those perennial board issues. What do we do about nonmembers who show up to our services? Why should we let them get away with taking advantage of our shul without paying anything? And what can be done if they refuse to join?

Rabbi Shmuel bar Nachmeni offers a powerful answer to this conundrum. Who owns the city synagogue? Not the board. Not the members. Everyone. It is a public institution. Consequently, it must be open and available to all, whether or not they officially own it on paper or not. If the members don't have the power to sell the building, they probably shouldn't be dictating who davens there either.

Rabbi Herbert Goldstein, founder of the Institutional Synagogue in 1917 in Harlem understood this well. By the end of the first year, he had over a thousand members. What was his secret? Rabbi Goldstein felt that the synagogue should not cater to a select wealthy elite. The synagogue is for everybody. And so he sent the youth out going door to door, asking people to join the I.S., some paying as little as a dollar a year![1]

The truth is, he would have welcomed them without paying anything at all. But he didn't want them to feel bad and not end up attending because they couldn't afford to be members. And so he asked them to pay whatever they could, even a token amount if that's all they could—or would—pay.

So why pay synagogue dues if it's open to all anyway? Why be the *shlemazel* who pays full membership while everyone else gets a free ride? What is the point of being a shul member if you have no more rights or benefits than the nonmember sitting next you each morning at minyan?

The answer is that there's more to shul membership than paying for a place to daven. Purchasing a membership is like buying spiritual shares in the synagogue. You become a part owner and reap all the rewards of the success of the institution. Becoming a member means buying into the mission of the shul, which is to serve the entire community, as well as all who come from far and wide. Your membership entitles you to a share in every merit accrued by the organization. Every *tefillah*.

---

1   Reichel, *The Maverick Rabbi*.

Every word of Torah. Every act of *chessed* performed in the name of the congregation.

The board of directors of the shul are stewards of this public mitzvah institution. Think about any other charity or nonprofit board you sit on. You don't ask why you dedicate your time, efforts, and financial investment to the organization when other people just sit back and watch. You take pride in knowing that you are steering an incredible ship, a vehicle for Divine blessing. And that should be our attitude toward shul volunteerism. It doesn't matter whether or not anyone else steps up. The more you are doing, the greater your spiritual merit.

Shuls are for everyone. Open your doors and your hearts. When you invite kids—whose parents won't join the shul—to be part of the shul's youth program, you become their spiritual parents. When you invite people in to daven even when they haven't paid for a seat, you maximize Hashem's blessing, which should be more than sufficient motivation. May you partner with Hashem in tending to the spiritual needs of all His children!

Fashionably Early

King David was growing old and it was clear that his life was drawing to a close. But who would be the successor to the throne? His son Adoniyah began boasting, "I will be king!" He provided himself with chariots and horses, and an entourage of fifty men. His father never scolded him, "Why did you do that?" He was the one born after Avshalom and, like him, was very handsome. He conferred with Yoav ben Tzeruyah and with the priest Evyasar, and they supported Adoniyah. But the priest Tzadok, Benayahu ben Yehoyada, the prophet Nosson, Shim'i and Re'i, and David's own fighting men did not side with Adoniyah. Adoniyah made a sacrificial feast of sheep, oxen, and fattened calves at the Zocheles stone, which is near En-Rogel. He invited all his brothers and all the king's courtiers of the tribe of Yehudah. But he did not invite the prophet Nosson, or Benayahu, or the fighting men, or his brother Shlomo.

Then Nosson said to Batsheva, Shlomo's mother, "You must have heard that Adoniyah has assumed the kingship without the knowledge of our lord David. Now take my advice, so that you may save your life and the life of your son, Shlomo. Go immediately to King David and say to him, 'Did not you, O lord, king, swear to your maidservant: "Your son, Shlomo, shall succeed me as king, and he shall sit upon my throne?" Then why has Adoniyah become king?' While you are still there talking with the king, I will come in after you and confirm your words."

So, Batsheva went to the king in his chamber. She bowed low in homage to the king, and the king asked, "What troubles you?" She answered him, "My lord, you yourself swore to your maidservant by Hashem your God: 'Your son, Shlomo, shall succeed me as king, and he shall sit upon my throne.' Yet now Adoniyah has become king, and you, my lord, the king, know nothing about it. He has prepared a sacrificial feast of a great many oxen, fattened calves, and sheep, and he has invited all the king's sons and Evyasar the priest and Yoav commander of the army; but he has not invited your servant Shlomo. And so, the eyes of all Israel are upon you, O lord, king, to tell them who shall succeed my lord, the king, on the throne. Otherwise, when my lord, the king, lies down with his fathers, my son Shlomo and I will be regarded as traitors."

She was still talking to the king when the prophet Nosson arrived. They announced to the king, "The prophet Nosson is here," and he entered the king's presence. Bowing low to the king with his face to the ground, Nosson said, "O lord, king, you must have said, 'Adoniyah shall succeed me as king and he shall sit upon my throne.' For he has gone down today and prepared a sacrificial feast of a great many oxen, fatlings, and sheep. He invited all the king's sons and the army officers and Evyasar the priest. At this very moment they are eating and drinking with him, and they are shouting, 'Long live King Adoniyah!' But he did not invite me your servant, or the priest Tzadok, or Benayahu ben Yehoyada, or your servant Shlomo. Can this decision have come from my lord, the king, without your telling your servant who is to succeed to the throne of my lord, the king?"

King David's responded, "Summon Batsheva!" She reentered the king's presence and stood before the king. And the king took an oath, saying, "As Hashem lives, who has rescued me from every trouble: The oath I swore to you by Hashem, God of Israel, that your son, Shlomo, should succeed me as king and that he should sit upon my throne in my stead, I will fulfill this very day!" Batsheva bowed low in homage to the king with her face to the ground, and she said, "May my lord, King David, live forever!" Then King David said, "Summon to me the priest Tzadok, the prophet Nosson, and Benayahu ben Yehoyada."

When they came before the king, the king said to them, "Take my loyal soldiers, and have my son Shlomo ride on my mule and bring him down to Gichon. Let the priest Tzadok and the prophet Nosson anoint him there king over Israel, whereupon you shall sound the horn and shout, 'Long live Shlomo HaMelech!' Then march up after him and let him come in and sit on my throne. For he shall succeed me as king; him I designate to be ruler of Israel and Yehudah." Benayahu ben Yehoyada spoke up and said to the king, "Amen! And may Hashem, the God of my lord, the king, so ordain. As Hashem was with my lord, the king, so may He be with Shlomo; and may He exalt his throne even higher than the throne of my lord, King David."[1]

שָׁאֲלוּ תַּלְמִידָיו אֶת רַבִּי פְּרִידָא בַּמֶּה הֶאֱרַכְתָּ יָמִים אָמַר לָהֶם מִיָּמַי לֹא קְדָמַנִי אָדָם לְבֵית הַמִּדְרָשׁ וְלֹא בֵּרַכְתִּי לִפְנֵי כֹהֵן וְלֹא אָכַלְתִּי מִבְּהֵמָה שֶׁלֹּא הוּרְמוּ מַתְּנוֹתֶיהָ.

Rabbi Pereida was once asked by his disciples: In the merit of which virtue were you blessed with longevity? He said to them: In all my days, no person ever arrived before me to the study hall. And I never led bentching in the presence of a Kohen. And I never ate from an animal whose gifts were not elevated.

Should a person strive to be the first to do a mitzvah? Rabbi Pereida teaches that it all depends on the nature of the mitzvah. Sometimes you should run to be the first. Other times call for humility and the acknowledgment that you need to wait your turn. Being the first in shul or the *beis midrash* each morning is undoubtedly admirable. But always running to be the first at the *amud*, to lead services, not so much.

When it comes to a mitzvah that many people can participate in equally, then it makes sense to do one's very best to lead the way and demonstrate your passion to be the first off the mark. But for those mitzvos that only allow space for one individual, it's always preferable to see who else might deserve or need the honor more than you.

---

1   *Melachim I*, chap. 1.

What is the meaning of Rabbi Pereida's third merit? Literally, he is referring to the parts of an animal that are designated as priestly gifts. He would always confirm those gifts were separated prior to partaking of the meat placed before him. But, on a deeper level, perhaps Rabbi Pereida was suggesting that he was in control of his trait of swiftness throughout his life. Lest we attribute his daily alacrity to a natural impulsiveness, he tells us that he would sit down to a meal and think about the meat in front of him. What was its purpose? What was his purpose in consuming it? And he would elevate its Heavenly gifts.

The kashrus of the food we ingest is only the first level of its sanctification. The second level entails making the right *berachos* before and after the food. The third, and ultimate level requires consuming the food for the right reasons. If we eat in the pursuit of our physical desire for pleasure or even merely to satisfy our hunger, we limit the potential of this food. When we eat, however, to gain strength to serve Heaven, the food attains its ultimate level of perfection. Rabbi Pereida's consumption accomplished the highest level of sanctification possible for the piece of meat he was served. But the only way to ensure that is the case is to stop and think before consuming any item of this world.

So, what was the secret of Rabbi Pereida's longevity? It was his mastery over speed. Number 1: He was always the first to arrive in shul or to raise his hand to do a mitzvah. Number 2: In his haste, he would never try to beat someone else to a position where someone else may have felt slighted. And number 3: His alacrity didn't imply impetuousness. He was quick, but thoughtful. Eager, but circumspect.

The *Ramchal* lists the attribute of *zerizus*, alacrity, as a key character trait one must endeavor to attain.[2] But what's the point of *zerizus*? Why should you strive for alacrity in life? Is there anything better about being the first person at minyan than being the tenth man? Either way you've made the minyan and facilitated the communal prayer!

And so the *Ramchal* offers the story of Shlomo HaMelech's coronation as an example of what might go wrong as we set out toward our desired

---

2   *Mesillas Yesharim*, chap. 6.

destinations in life.[3] Our Sages teach that Gichon was right around the corner and should have been reachable in no time at all. But even brief journeys can end up taking forever when we aren't swift to the mark. Due to a lack of *zerizus*, Shlomo almost lost the throne.[4]

And that's the distinction Rabbi Pereida felt about his daily *zerizus*. It is a big deal to always be in shul first, especially when contrasted with the daily latecomer. Nobody ever plans to arrive late, but unexpected things happen. You might encounter traffic jams along the way, or someone might stop you to chat, or, just as you're leaving, your child suddenly asks you to pour some cereal for him. And before you know it, all your plans to get to shul right on time have culminated in your late entry—once again. Meanwhile, the Rabbi Pereida-type who lives twenty minutes away always manages to be wearing his tallis and tefillin before the minyan has even arrived.

The clock in the Lambeau Field stadium in Green Bay, Wisconsin, is always fifteen minutes ahead of schedule. It faces Lombardi Avenue, named for the famous football coach who led the Green Bay Packers to victory in the early 1960s. Vince Lombardi insisted that the players be at every practice at least fifteen minutes early. If they arrived fourteen minutes early, they were sent home. Before long, "Lombardi Time" became the gold standard for sports and business coaches alike.

Of course, in our tradition, we have a different name for it. It's called "Rabbi Pereida Time," in tribute to Rabbi Pereida who was always the first in shul every morning. If you want to master the attribute of *zerizus*, you need to live on Rabbi Pereida Time. If you plan to arrive exactly on time, you're setting yourself up for failure. Or, at the very least, you're creating unnecessary stress and anxiety in your life. Because, inevitably, something will come up along the way to Gichon that will stall you and delay your arrival. When you plan to be there on Rabbi Pereida Time, what's the worst that can happen? You arrive a few minutes early and have to learn a little extra Gemara while you're waiting for *Shacharis* to begin?

---

3   Ibid., chap. 8.

4   *Bereishis Rabbah* 76:2.

Life is full of traffic jams. But when you operate on Rabbi Pereida Time, catching an extra red light or two doesn't faze you. You'll still be the first one in shul. May you always strive for *zerizus*!

Beneath Your Dignity

vremel was a recently married student of Rav Mordechai Gifter. One day he approached the rabbi complaining of marriage problems.

"*Rebbi*, we're having issues. She wants me to take out the trash."

"*Nu*, so what's the problem?" Rav Gifter inquired of the young man.

"Well, I'm a *kollel yungerman* and I think it's a little beneath me to be seen dealing with the trash."

"You certainly make a good point," agreed the rabbi. "If you feel it's beneath your dignity, you shouldn't do it." Happy that his teacher understood him, the fellow returned home to let his wife know that Rav Gifter had agreed with his position.

The next morning at 7:45 AM, the doorbell rings. Still in his pajamas, Avremel opens the door to find Rav Gifter standing on the doorstep.

"*Rebbi*! What's going on? Is there some kind of emergency at the yeshiva?"

"No, no emergency, *baruch Hashem*," replies the teacher, "I'm here to take out your garbage. I understand that you feel it's beneath your dignity to take it out. That's okay. But somebody must do it!"[1]

---

1   Horowitz, *Otzar Sippurim L'Mechanchim* 2:386.

שָׁאֲלוּ תַּלְמִידָיו אֶת רַבִּי נְחוּנְיָא בֶּן הַקָּנָה בַּמֶּה הֶאֱרַכְתָּ יָמִים אָמַר לָהֶם מִיָּמַי
לֹא נִתְכַּבַּדְתִּי בִּקְלוֹן חֲבֵרִי וְלֹא עָלְתָה עַל מִטָּתִי קִלְלַת חֲבֵרִי וַוַתְּרָן בְּמָמוֹנִי
הָיִיתִי לֹא נִתְכַּבַּדְתִּי בִּקְלוֹן חֲבֵרִי כִּי הָא דְּרַב הוּנָא דָּרֵי מָרָא אַכַּתְפֵיהּ אֲתָא
רַב חָנָא בַּר חֲנִילַאי וְקָא דָּרֵי מִינֵּיהּ אֲמַר לֵיהּ אִי רְגִילַתְּ דְּדָרֵית בְּמָאתָיִךְ דְּרִי
וְאִי לָא אִתְיַיקּוֹרֵי אֲנָא בְּזִילוּתָא דִידָךְ לָא נִיחָא לִי וְלֹא עָלְתָה עַל מִטָּתִי
קִלְלַת חֲבֵרִי כִּי הָא דְּמַר זוּטְרָא כִּי הֲוָה סָלֵיק לְפוּרְיֵיהּ אֲמַר שְׁרֵי לֵיהּ לְכָל
מַאן דְּצַעֲרָן וַוַתְּרָן בְּמָמוֹנִי הָיִיתִי דְּאָמַר מָר אִיּוֹב וַוַתְּרָן בְּמָמוֹנֵיהּ הֲוָה שֶׁהָיָה
מַנִּיחַ פְּרוּטָה לַחֶנְוָנִי מִמָּמוֹנֵיהּ.

Rabbi Nechunya ben Hakaneh's students asked him: How did you lengthen your days? He replied: I never sought honor at the expense of anyone else; the curse of others did not come upon my bed; and I was liberal with my money. "I never sought honor at the expense of anyone else" is like the time Rav Huna was carrying a spade on his shoulders. Rabbi Chana bar Chanilai entered and offered to carry it for him. Rav Huna said to him: If you regularly schlep such items back home, then by all means, carry it. But, if not, it is not appropriate that I should be honored via your degradation. "The curse of others did not come upon my bed" may be understood with reference to Mar Zutra. Before he would lay down to sleep, he would say: I hereby forgive all who troubled me today. "And I was liberal with my money," as Mar taught: Iyov was liberal with his money, for he would leave a tip for service with every merchant.

What's the secret of a long life? We don't necessarily know how many years Rabbi Nechunya lived, but here he teaches us how he lengthened his days—what made each day exciting, invigorating, and worth living.

First, he never felt that any task was beneath his dignity. When you view every other human being as a *tzelem Elokim*—created in the image of God—how could you ever feel your dignity is any worthier than any other person's? That attitude is so enriching. Suddenly greeting your garbage collector is just as meaningful as greeting the president! Everyone is noble and, therefore, a pleasure and an honor with whom to interact.

Second, he would never go to bed angry. Many married couples are familiar with this technique, but how many of us utilize the method for all our relationships and interactions? Imagine how different your life would be if you never went to bed upset with anyone! Often our lives are weighed down by unresolved conflicts. Issues with colleagues, neighbors, parents, siblings, children. If you could dispose of those issues each night, think about how your life would be completely refreshed and reinvigorated each day.

But, you say, how can I resolve the issues if the other person isn't present? The answer is that before you can make peace with another individual, you must find peace within yourself. If you're still angry with that person, you won't be able to resolve anything. Only once you've forgiven him in your heart, will you be able to see things from his perspective and resolve matters with him. And if he chooses to be obstinate, then he'll have to live with the discomfort of unresolved issues. You can remove the burden from your heart and simply shower him with kindness.

Third, he would always leave a tip. Leaving a tip tells the service-provider that you really appreciate his efforts. A tip is not about the money. It's about showing the other person that you honor him as your fellow human being—that you don't view him as someone there to wait on you. You value the assistance he has provided for you. A tip is a nod to his importance in your life. It's a morale boost for both parties.

And Rabbi Nechunya saw giving a tip as an expression of being liberal with his money. When you recognize that your material possessions come from the Almighty, you understand that they've been given to you to make this world physically and emotionally a better place. There's no reason to be stingy with your blessings. Hashem wants you to utilize the bounty He has given you to bring joy to others. The more liberally you tip, the more generous you train yourself to be, and the more you'll come to realize that everything comes from Heaven.

Rabbi Nechunya's secret to a happy life was treating everyone with dignity, never remaining aggravated, and not stressing over money matters. That's how he lengthened his days.

Stop stressing over your honor. Stop stressing over your finances. Before you go to bed tonight, forgive anyone who might have wronged you. May you find happiness in treating everyone as a child of Hashem and every penny as a gift from Hashem to be shared with His children!

Shuls vs. Gardens

I f you never witnessed the ancient Great Synagogue of Alexandria, you never saw the glory of Israel. Its structure was like a large basilica boasting a colonnade within a colonnade. At times there were over a million people in attendance—six hundred thousand and another six hundred thousand, twice the number of those who left Egypt. The sanctuary contained seventy-one golden chairs, corresponding to the seventy-one members of the Great Sanhedrin, each of which consisted of no less than twenty-one thousand talents of gold!

In the center of the shul stood a wooden platform. The *shammes* would stand upon it, with scarves in his hand. Because the shul was so large and the people could not always hear the chazzan, when he reached the conclusion of a *berachah*, the *shammes* waved a scarf and all the people would respond amen.

But it was so much more than just a place to pray. The members of the various crafts would sit together: the goldsmiths would sit among themselves, the silversmiths among themselves, the blacksmiths among themselves, the coppersmiths among themselves, and the weavers among themselves. And when a new person arrived, he would recognize people who plied his craft, and he would join them in their section. And, from there, he would secure his livelihood as well as the livelihood of the members of his household, as his colleagues would find him work in the business.[1]

דָּרֵשׁ רָבָא מַאי דִּכְתִיב ה' מָעוֹן אַתָּה הָיִיתָ לָנוּ אֵלּוּ בָּתֵּי כְנֵסִיּוֹת וּבָתֵּי מִדְרָשׁוֹת אָמַר אַבָּיֵי מֵרִישׁ הֲוַאי גְּרֵיסְנָא בְּבֵיתָא וּמְצַלֵּינָא בְּבֵי כְנִשְׁתָּא כֵּיוָן דִּשְׁמַעִית לְהָא דְּקָאָמַר דָּוִד ה' אָהַבְתִּי מְעוֹן בֵּיתֶךָ הֲוַאי גְּרֵיסְנָא בְּבֵי כְנִשְׁתָּא תַּנְיָא רַבִּי אֶלְעָזָר הַקַּפָּר אוֹמֵר עֲתִידִין בָּתֵּי כְנֵסִיּוֹת וּבָתֵּי מִדְרָשׁוֹת שֶׁבְּבָבֶל שֶׁיִּקָּבְעוּ בְּאֶרֶץ יִשְׂרָאֵל שֶׁנֶּאֱמַר כִּי כְתָבוֹר בֶּהָרִים וּכְכַרְמֶל בַּיָּם יָבֹא וַהֲלֹא דְּבָרִים קַל וָחוֹמֶר וּמָה תָּבוֹר וְכַרְמֶל שֶׁלֹּא בָּאוּ אֶלָּא לְפִי שָׁעָה לִלְמוֹד תּוֹרָה נִקְבָּעִים בְּאֶרֶץ יִשְׂרָאֵל בָּתֵּי כְנֵסִיּוֹת וּבָתֵּי מִדְרָשׁוֹת שֶׁקּוֹרִין וּמַרְבִּיצִין בָּהֶן תּוֹרָה עַל אַחַת כַּמָּה וְכַמָּה.

Rava expounded: What is the meaning of, "Lord, You have been our dwelling place"? This is referring to the shul and beis midrash. Abaye said: Initially, I used to learn Torah in my home and daven in shul. But once I heard that which David says, "Lord, I love the habitation of Your house," I would always learn Torah in shul. It is taught: Rabbi Elazar HaKappar says: In the future, the shuls and batei midrash in Babylonia will be reestablished in Eretz Yisrael, as it is states, "Surely, like Tavor among the mountains, and like Carmel by the sea, so shall he come." And these matters are inferred through an a fortiori argument: Just as Tavor and Carmel, which came only momentarily to study Torah [at Sinai], were relocated and established in Eretz Yisrael in reward for their actions, all the more so should the shuls and study halls, in which the Torah is read and disseminated, be relocated.

Why daven in shul? Isn't Hashem everywhere? He is available and can be encountered whether you are at home or at an office *Minchah* minyan or in your neighbor's garden minyan!

A shul is not just a place to daven. As Abaye discovers in our Gemara, the shul is the earthly abode of the Almighty. That may be difficult to comprehend. After all, why would Hashem need a physical dwelling

---

1   *Sukkah* 51b.

place? And the truth is, He doesn't, but, following the sin of the Golden Calf, He noted *our* need for a tangible locus of prayer, and He instructed us to build the Tabernacle. With the destruction of the Temple, our shuls were imbued with a ray of its former sanctity.

This sanctity has profound ramifications. A shul may not be sold for mundane purposes. One may not use the shul as a shortcut. There are various halachos and *minhagim* concerning the proper design of a shul, such as the directive to place the *bimah* in the center or the specific measurement of the *mechitzah*. The halachos of an ad hoc minyan are far more flexible because the venue lacks the *kedushas Beis Mikdash Me'at*, the sanctity of the miniature Temple, manifest in a shul.

And then there are countless intangibles and outgrowths of shul life. The Great Synagogue of Alexandria offers the example of professional networking that synagogue communities offer. Of course, that's not the primary purpose of a shul. But something magical happens when we gather together in a central location to worship our Father in Heaven. In the words of Shlomo HaMelech, *"B'rov am hadras Melech"* —we glorify the King when we gather as a multitude of people.[2]

Yes, you can daven anywhere. But shul life provides so much more than just a place to daven. In the prayer we recite each Shabbos before *Mussaf*, we declare:

> *May He who blessed our fathers Avraham, Yitzchak, and Yaakov bless this entire holy congregation along with all other holy congregations: them, their wives, their sons and daughters, all that is theirs. May He bless those who designate synagogues for prayer and those who come there to pray, those who provide lamps for light and wine for Kiddush and Havdalah, food for visitors and charity for the poor, and all who faithfully occupy themselves with the needs of the community. May the Holy One, blessed be He, give them reward; may He remove from them all illness, grant them complete healing, and forgive their sins. May He send blessing and success to all the work of*

---

2   *Mishlei* 14:28.

their hands, together with all Israel their brethren, and let us
say amen.

Listen to all the details covered in this prayer. When I hear the blessings we request for the men, women, sons, and daughters, I picture
a community replete with davening and learning opportunities for men
and women, youth and children's services. When I hear the blessings
we ask for those providing light, wine, food, and charity, I picture
a community that incorporates active *chessed* initiatives. All of these
elements are integral to shul life. A shul is not just a minyan in a fancy
building. It's the foundation of Jewish life.

And finally, Rabbi Elazar HaKappar's prophecy regarding the future
of our shuls should seal the deal when we're contemplating where to
daven. When Mashiach comes, all our shuls will be transported to
Yerushalayim. May you make yourself at home in the shul or *beis mid-*
rash now and for all eternity!

Path of Most Resistance

The author of *Lecha Dodi*, Rabbi Shlomo Alkabetz, was a disciple of Rabbi Yosef Karo long before they made the great journey from Turkey to Tzefas, Israel. One Shavuos, they decided to honor the Kabbalistic practice of staying up all night learning Torah. From dusk to dawn, not an idle word was uttered, as their lips never ceased from the sweet words of Torah.

Their goal was to review the entire *Torah She'bichsav* and *Torah She'baal Peh*, and, by midnight, they had already covered two orders of the Mishnah. Suddenly, from Rabbi Karo's mouth, an angel began to speak: "Listen my beloved friends," came the Heavenly voice. "You are very careful in your mitzvos. Peace unto you. You are praiseworthy and your parents are praised. You are fortunate in this world and fortunate in the World to Come. The words of your Torah have pierced the very Heavens, ascending directly to the Almighty. All the angels are silent, as the Holy One, blessed be He, is attentive to your voices. You shall now ascend to the Land of Israel where you will partake of the holy land's bounty!"

And on that night, the holy gathering repaired the breach that was caused when the B'nei Yisrael did not arise with alacrity on the morning of *Matan Torah*.[1]

---

1   Adapted from *Shelah, Aseres Hadibros: Shavuos, Ner Mitzvah*.

בְּשְׁנִיָּה זָכוֹר וְכוּ' אִיתְּמַר פּוּרִים שֶׁחָל לִהְיוֹת בְּעֶרֶב שַׁבָּת רַב אָמַר מַקְדִּימִין
פָּרָשַׁת זָכוֹר וּשְׁמוּאֵל אָמַר מְאַחֲרִין רַב אָמַר מַקְדִּימִין כִּי הֵיכִי דְּלָא תִּיקְדּוֹם
עֲשִׂיָּה לִזְכִירָה וּשְׁמוּאֵל אָמַר מְאַחֲרִין אָמַר לָךְ כֵּיוָן דְּאִיכָּא מוּקָּפִין דְּעָבְדִי
בַּחֲמֵיסָר עֲשִׂיָּה וּזְכִירָה בַּהֲדֵי הֲדֵי קָא אָתְיָין.

On the second, we read Zachor: It was stated: With regard to
when Purim occurs on a Friday, Rav said: The congregation
advances the reading of the portion of Zachor to the previous
Shabbos. And Shmuel said: They defer it to the Shabbos
following Purim. Rav said: They advance it, in order that the
observance of Purim should not precede the remembrance
[of Amalek]. And Shmuel said: They defer it. He would say
to you: Since there are the walled cities that observe Purim
on the fifteenth, the observance and the remembrance come
simultaneously.

The Mishnah discusses the four special Shabbos Torah readings
around Purim. "On the second Shabbos, we read *Zachor*," which
reminds us of our obligation to destroy Amalek. Amalek was the anti-
Semitic ancestor of Haman, who first attempted to destroy our people
when we left Egypt. His descendants have continued their attempts at
our destruction throughout the generations. Consequently, *Zachor* is
always read on the Shabbos prior to Purim to provide the background
and context.

According to Rav, *Zachor* is always read on the Shabbos before Purim,
even if the festival falls on Friday, since the *Megillah* states, "These days
shall be remembered and performed." If we were to celebrate Purim and
then subsequently read *Zachor*, the performance (of the festival) would
precede the remembrance (of the causal events) and would run counter
to the order of the verse.

But isn't that contrary to our general approach of *naaseh v'nishma*?
We take pride in our distinctive response to Hashem when He offered
us the Torah. On that momentous occasion, we committed ourselves
to the performance of His precepts prior to any intellectual inquiry!
Why in this instance does Rav insist that the understanding precede
our performance?

The answer lies in the contrast between *naaseh* and *nishma. Naaseh* represents doing what is difficult. *Nishma* represents the contentment one feels when given the chance to come to terms with the actions. The principle of *naaseh* prior to *nishma* means always tackling the tougher elements first. Success in life, whether spiritual or material, most often comes down to dealing with the difficult duties before engaging in the more palatable, agreeable experiences. The difference between successful people and unsuccessful people is the simple fact that some are willing to take the tough road while others seek the easy choices in life.

Generally, when it comes to mitzvos that we don't understand like keeping kosher or *bris milah*, our approach must be *naaseh v'nishma* — we will perform the mitzvos immediately even though we don't comprehend their ultimate purpose. Only once we've accepted the challenge of mitzvah performance do we then start delving into the whys and wherefores in an effort to satisfy our intellectual curiosity. And even then, some mitzvos will be more fathomable than others.

But then we have certain mitzvos that require very little convincing. Those are the naturally exciting and enjoyable mitzvos. Everyone loves doing Purim. We get dressed up. We have a big feast. We shake our *graggers*. We send gifts to one another.

After all this, who would want to hear a Torah reading like *Zachor* that makes nearly incomprehensible theological demands upon us? First, we must grapple with the implications of Purim — that anti-Semitism is a real and ever-present danger — and only subsequently may we celebrate the victory and miracle of our people's continued existence.

The *nishma*, in this case, poses a greater challenge than the *naaseh*, and therefore the remembrance must precede the performance. Only once we have faced our fears and insecurities, have we earned the right to revel in the mitzvah.

Indeed, that's true of many of our festivals. We love the Pesach Seder. But before we get to the "fun" bits, we must spend weeks cleaning our homes. And even when we finally reach the Seder table, we must "sing for our supper." We spend considerable time and effort investing in the narrative before we allow ourselves to feast.

Likewise, Sukkos is the "time of our rejoicing." But first, we must work for it. We toil to build a sukkah, and only then may we enjoy its shade. And even Shavuos isn't just about flowers and cheesecake. First, we must stay up all night learning, so we feel we have earned our joyful celebration of the Torah.[2]

In every field and endeavor throughout your life, your success depends on your willingness to tackle the big challenges head-on. To feel the "pain" before the "gain." If everything feels too easy to you, you need to ask yourself if you're avoiding the challenges.

Each time you make a choice, every time you prioritize your tasks, ask yourself which is the greater challenge. And that's the one you should aim to do first. Once you've tackled the challenging tasks, your long-term rewards are guaranteed to be far greater.

May you forever have the courage to choose the path of most resistance!

---

2   Rabbi J. Sacks, *Future Tense*, p. 66.

Is the Friend of the Nebach a Nebach?

Rabbi Shlomo Zalman Auerbach once arrived at a *chuppah* to be *mesader kiddushin*, the officiating rabbi. As everyone stood at the *chuppah*, the two *eidim*, the witnesses for the *kiddushin*, were called up. Suddenly, the rabbi found himself in a bit of a quandary. He happened to know one of the witnesses personally and knew that he would not be acceptable as a kosher *eid*. But there they were standing in front of all the guests. If he were to say something then and there, he would cause embarrassment all around.

Of course, no challenge ever confounded the great Rav Shlomo Zalman. He turned to the man and quietly asked him for a huge favor. "My dear friend, my voice is a little weak today. I'm afraid they won't hear me make the *berachos*. Do you mind if we switch places? You recite the *berachos* and I'll take your place here by the side."

"But, but, *rebbi*," stammered the young man, "I'm not a rabbi. I've never..." But Rav Shlomo Zalman insisted and went to get the man a siddur, just in case.

And indeed, that young couple had an illustrious witness for their wedding, the likes of which very few people ever merited—the great, and exceedingly humble, Rav Shlomo Zalman Auerbach![1]

אָמַר רַבִּי יוֹחָנָן כָּל מָקוֹם שֶׁאַתָּה מוֹצֵא גְּבוּרָתוֹ שֶׁל הַקָּדוֹשׁ בָּרוּךְ הוּא אַתָּה מוֹצֵא עַנְוְתָנוּתוֹ דָּבָר זֶה כָּתוּב בַּתּוֹרָה וְשָׁנוּי בַּנְּבִיאִים וּמְשׁוּלָשׁ בַּכְּתוּבִים כָּתוּב בַּתּוֹרָה כִּי ה׳ אֱלֹקֵיכֶם הוּא אֱלֹקֵי הָאֱלֹהִים וַאֲדֹנֵי הָאֲדֹנִים וּכְתִיב בַּתְרֵיהּ עֹשֶׂה מִשְׁפַּט יָתוֹם וְאַלְמָנָה שָׁנוּי בַּנְּבִיאִים כֹּה אָמַר רָם וְנִשָּׂא שׁוֹכֵן עַד וְקָדוֹשׁ וְגוֹ׳ וּכְתִיב בַּתְרֵיהּ וְאֶת דַּכָּא וּשְׁפַל רוּחַ מְשׁוּלָשׁ בַּכְּתוּבִים דִּכְתִיב סֹלּוּ לָרֹכֵב בָּעֲרָבוֹת בְּיָ-הּ שְׁמוֹ וּכְתִיב בַּתְרֵיהּ אֲבִי יְתוֹמִים וְדַיַּן אַלְמָנוֹת.

Rabbi Yochanan taught: Wherever you find mentioned in the Torah the power of the Holy One, blessed be He, you also find His humility mentioned. This fact is stated in the Torah, repeated in Neviim, and stated a third time in Kesuvim. It is written in the Torah, "For Hashem your God, He is the God of gods and Lord of lords," and it says immediately afterward, "He performs justice for the fatherless and widow." It is repeated in Neviim, "For thus says the High and Lofty One, Who inhabits eternity and Whose name is holy," and it says immediately afterward, "I am with him that is of a contrite and humble spirit." It is stated a third time in Kesuvim, as it is written, "Extol him that rides upon the Heavens, whose name is the Lord," and immediately afterward it is written, "Father of orphans and a judge of widows."

Who is powerful? What defines greatness? We think of greatness and power in terms of control—the more material and physical resources one controls, the more powerful one is. We also think of greatness and power in terms of knowledge—the more intelligence a person exhibits, the more powerful that individual is.

That's not the Torah's conception of power. How do you recognize power and greatness? In he who is humble. The tough character who

---

1 Horowitz, *Otzar Hasippurim L'Mechanchim* 1:371.

needs to push his weight around and bully others is not great. Nor is the person who needs to brandish his knowledge to prove his superiority.

Greatness, says the Gemara, is to be found in the ability to protect and care.

The Talmud equates this power to protect with humility. The Almighty's true power is to be found in His humility. And His humility is to be found in His loving-kindness and care for the most downtrodden. Hashem knows everything, but that's not what makes Him great. His greatness lies in the fact that He humbles Himself and expresses that knowledge in His care for His creatures.

And that's what He wants from us. Certainly, we must learn as much Torah as possible. But if it doesn't lead to humility and loving-kindness, we have missed the point of all the knowledge we've labored for. True power and greatness means lowering yourself from that intense level of information and being prepared to serve the world. Shlomo HaMelech composed three thousand parables,[2] meaning that in order to bring down his extraordinary wisdom to the level of the layperson, he needed to compose a parable within a parable within a parable to the power of three thousand![3]

One of the leading institutions in the field of Jewish education in America is Yeshivas Chofetz Chaim. What makes graduates of the yeshiva so awe-inspiring is their humble commitment to *chinuch*. What makes their dedication so extraordinary? In order to get *semichah* from the yeshiva, it takes about ten years. But then there's an expectation that the graduates of the yeshiva will teach children, at all levels of school education. So you have many incredible *talmidei chachamim* who have sat and learned in yeshiva and *kollel* for over a decade, and then they go off to teach *alef-beis* to five-year olds. Now, that's humility of the highest Divine order!

True greatness is the ability to "lower" oneself and engage with every individual regardless of his age, level of learning, observance, and financial or social status. It's only those who are insecure who feel the

---

2   *Melachim I* 5:12.

3   *Baal Shem Tov Hashalem (Pe'er Mikedoshim)*, p. 393.

need to prove themselves by only talking to certain people or mixing in certain crowds. When you're confident and comfortable in your own skin, you never feel ashamed or embarrassed to be caught talking to the person everyone else considers the *"nebach"* or the *"shlemazel."* After all, why would you? That's the person with whom the Almighty Himself is spending time!

And the truth is, when you're really a great person, you don't even understand what those other people are talking about. That fellow they call the *nebach* is actually quite an interesting, wonderful person, if they'd simply take the time to get to know him. May you achieve greatness by never hesitating to spend time with the people with whom Hashem is friends!

Pesukei D'Zimrah
Is the Gelilah of Davening

n the early days of the Lakewood Yeshiva, one of the major benefactors once made a bold comment to Rabbi Aharon Kotler, the founding Rosh Yeshiva:

"*Rebbi*, I'm supporting your yeshiva and so I have an equal merit in the reward for the learning, right?"

"That's correct," replied Rabbi Kotler. "We have a partnership just like the one that existed between Yissachar and Zevulun. You provide the material needs, I provide the spiritual needs, and we share the reward in *Olam Haba*."

"So how are you and I any different, *rebbi*?" the man smirked, "We'll both end up in the same place!"

"The difference between us," responded the Rosh Yeshiva, "is that while we may both have a wonderful *Olam Haba* in store for us, I also have an *Olam Hazeh*!"

אָמַר רַבִּי שְׁפַטְיָה אָמַר רַבִּי יוֹחָנָן הַגּוֹלֵל סֵפֶר תּוֹרָה צָרִיךְ שֶׁיַּעֲמִידֶנּוּ עַל
הַתֶּפֶר וְאָמַר וְאָמַר רַבִּי שְׁפַטְיָה אָמַר רַבִּי יוֹחָנָן הַגּוֹלֵל סֵפֶר תּוֹרָה גּוֹלְלוֹ מִבַּחוּץ
וְאֵין גּוֹלְלוֹ מִבִּפְנִים מְהַדְּקוֹ מְהַדְּקוֹ מִבִּפְנִים וּכְשֶׁהוּא מְהַדְּקוֹ מְהַדְּקוֹ מִבִּפְנִים וְאֵינוֹ מְהַדְּקוֹ מִבַּחוּץ
וְאָמַר רַבִּי שְׁפַטְיָה אָמַר רַבִּי יוֹחָנָן עֲשָׂרָה שֶׁקְּרָאוּ בַּתּוֹרָה הַגָּדוֹל שֶׁבָּהֶם גּוֹלֵל
סֵפֶר תּוֹרָה הַגּוֹלְלוֹ נוֹטֵל שָׂכָר כּוּלָּן דְּאָמַר רַבִּי יְהוֹשֻׁעַ בֶּן לֵוִי עֲשָׂרָה שֶׁקְּרָאוּ

בַּתּוֹרָה הַגּוֹלֵל סֵפֶר תּוֹרָה קִיבֵּל שָׂכָר כּוּלָן שָׂכָר כּוּלָן שָׂכָר כּוּלָן סָלְקָא דַעְתָּךְ אֶלָּא
אֵימָא קִיבֵּל שָׂכָר כְּנֶגֶד כּוּלָן.

Rabbi Shefatyah quoted Rabbi Yochanan: When one does gelilah, he needs to position it so that it closes on the seam between two sheets of parchment. And Rabbi Shefatyah quoted Rabbi Yochanan: If ten people read from the Torah, the greatest among them should do gelilah. And the one who does gelilah takes the reward of all of them, as Rabbi Yehoshua ben Levi said: If ten people read from the Torah, the one who does gelilah receives the reward of all of them. Can it enter your mind that he actually receives the reward of all of them? Rather, say: He receives a reward equivalent to that of all of them.

Rabbi Shefatyah teaches that the most important call-up is *gelilah*. Now, that's counterintuitive! Most people believe that *gelilah* is simply the consolation prize, given even to children. Some even like to joke that getting *gelilah* ranks alongside being asked to lead *Pesukei D'Zimrah*, the first part of davening, when people are still meandering into shul! What makes *gelilah* special?

The *Aruch Hashulchan* explains the importance of the *gelilah* recipient: He's the one who ensures that the Torah is not left open and unattended.[1] The *Bach* writes that the reason the *gelilah* honoree receives extra reward is because of all the extra laws with which he must be familiar.[2] These halachos and *minhagim* include the necessity of positioning the seam in the middle and ensuring the *Bereishis* side of the Torah is atop the *Devarim* side when the Torah is closed. There's more to *gelilah* than you think!

Actually, according to the *Mishnah Berurah*, nowadays we divide the classic *gelilah* ritual into the two honors of *hagbah* and *gelilah*, and the primary reward is reserved for the person who performs *hagbah*.[3] The *Ramban* interprets the verse "Cursed be the man who does not uphold

---

1   *Orach Chaim* 147:8.
2   *Orach Chaim* 147.
3   Ibid., 147:5.

the words of this Torah"[4] as an exhortation to the person doing *hagbah* to make sure everyone—men and women—can see the writing inside the Torah when he lifts it up and turns it around.[5] Getting *hagbah* right is so important that the *Chasam Sofer* suggests that it borders on a Biblical obligation![6]

That's why, far from *hagbah* and *gelilah* being the "bottom of the barrel" call-ups, they're actually the honors that are deserving of the highest reward. In a certain sense, they epitomize the aphorism, "Torah study is great as it leads to action."[7] The primary reward is reserved for the person who demonstrates the purpose of the Torah reading, manifesting it in action.

While we could spend hours discussing the distinction of *hagbah* and *gelilah*, let's be honest with ourselves. Everyone knows that *gelilah* is not *maftir*. If you've been doing a "proverbial *hagbah*" for some time now, it's time to ask yourself whether it might not be time for a "speaking part." It's cute to compare *Pesukei D'Zimrah* to *gelilah*, but the fact is the former takes effort and expertise. It entails getting to shul on time. It means knowing the right tunes for weekday, Shabbos, and *Yamim Nora'im* (yes, they're all different). And, of course, it requires a fluency that will get the congregation to *Yishtabach* in a timely manner.

I'm not talking *literally* about receiving an *aliyah* versus getting *hagbah* or *gelilah*. Unlike the *Pesukei D'Zimrah* analogy, almost everyone knows how to recite the *berachos* over the Torah. What I mean by "proverbial *hagbah*" is those areas of Yiddishkeit that are supporting-actor roles. Just like Rav Kotler chided the benefactor of the Lakewood Yeshiva, in Jewish life we have leading roles and supporting roles. They are, by no means, mutually exclusive—one should certainly aspire to fulfill both. But, while the *hagbah* role is to "uphold the words of this Torah," one must always maintain the hope and aspiration to bless the words of the Torah by devoting oneself to serious daily study.

---

4   *Devarim* 27:26.
5   Ibid., 4:44.
6   *Yoreh Deah* 276.
7   *Kiddushin* 40b.

Are you settling for spiritual mediocrity, satisfying yourself with tying up the Torah, as it were, after everyone else has finished reading it? No doubt, someone has to do it, but if it's always you, maybe it's time to move on and expect more from yourself. Doing *gelilah* may get you to the same final destination but imagine how rich and fulfilling your life would be if you were prepared to invest the time and effort into mastering real Torah knowledge in this world.

In *Olam Haba*, you don't want just to be in Heaven, you want to appreciate Heaven. The way to accomplish that goal is to achieve mastery of Hashem's wisdom in this world. All good people go to Heaven, but only those who have mastered the Torah are truly able to appreciate everything *Olam Haba* has to offer.

They tell the story of David, who was new to shul and offered *hagbah*. It was painful to watch. He could barely lift the *Sefer Torah*, almost dropped it, and sat down very quickly. Feeling very embarrassed about the episode, he resolved to go home and work out. For the next few months, he lifted weights and did push-ups, sit-ups, and pull-ups.

Finally, he felt ready to face the *kehillah* once more. The next Shabbos, off he went, pumped and all set to make amends. All of a sudden, he heard the *gabbai* call his name. He rushed up to the *bimah*, grabbed the *Sefer Torah*, lifted it and opened it up wide, showing ten columns of the Torah. He pivoted to the left and then to the right.

Proudly, he turned to the *gabbai* and said, "*Nu*, what do you think?"

"Wow, I must say, that *hagbah* was amazing," responded the *gabbai*, "but, I called you up for *shelishi*."

At some point, we must all graduate and demand of ourselves that we reach our greatest potential. While it's true that *hagbah* requires a proper understanding of the laws, don't ever settle for less than the very best. Now that you've mastered the art of "*hagbah*," it's time to aspire to "*shelishi*." May you toil in Torah today and be rewarded with spiritual bliss in this world and the next!

About the Author

Rabbi Daniel Friedman is currently on his fourth *daf yomi* cycle. He received *semichah yadin yadin* from Rav Gedalia Dov Schwartz, *zt"l*, Av Beis Din of the Beth Din of America. He has served communities in the US, Canada, Australia, and the UK. His articles have appeared in the *Journal of Halacha and Contemporary Society*, *YU Lamdan*, the *Jewish Press*, the *Jerusalem Post*, Aish.com, and numerous other outlets. He was the inaugural chair of the National Holocaust Monument of Canada and is a world-renowned expert on the intersection of halachah and international relations.

ABOUT THE AUTHOR

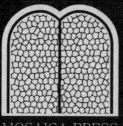

MOSAICA PRESS
BOOK PUBLISHERS

Elegant, Meaningful & Bold

info@MosaicaPress.com
www.MosaicaPress.com

The Mosaica Press team of
acclaimed editors and designers
is attracting some of the most
compelling thinkers and teachers
in the Jewish community today.
Our books are available around
the world.

HARAV YAACOV HABER
RABBI DORON KORNBLUTH